Nest in the Wind

NEST IN THE WIND

Adventures in Anthropology
on a Tropical Island

Martha C. Ward

University of New Orleans

WAVELAND

PRESS, INC.

Prospect Heights, Illinois

For information about this book, write or call:
Waveland Press, Inc.
P.O. Box 400
Prospect Heights, Illinois 60070
(312) 634-0081

Illustrations by Nancy Zoder Dawes

This book is dedicated to the men I love,
in particular

Dr. John L. Fischer
Anthropologist, mentor, colleague, and friend

and

Hugh Coonfield
Teacher, counselor, craftsman, and my father

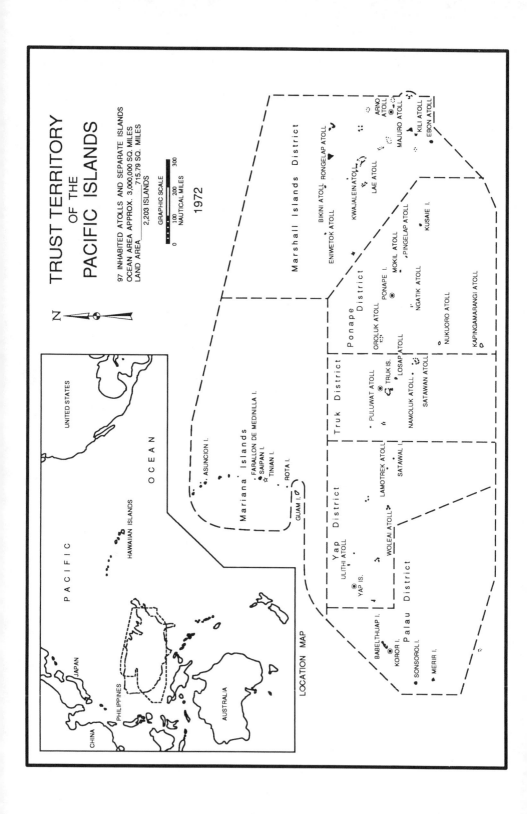

TRUST TERRITORY
OF THE
PACIFIC ISLANDS

97 INHABITED ATOLLS AND SEPARATE ISLANDS
OCEAN AREA APPROX. 3,000,000 SQ. MILES
LAND AREA   715.79 SQ. MILES
2,203 ISLANDS

GRAPHIC SCALE

0   100   200   300
NAUTICAL MILES

1972

LOCATION MAP

Contents

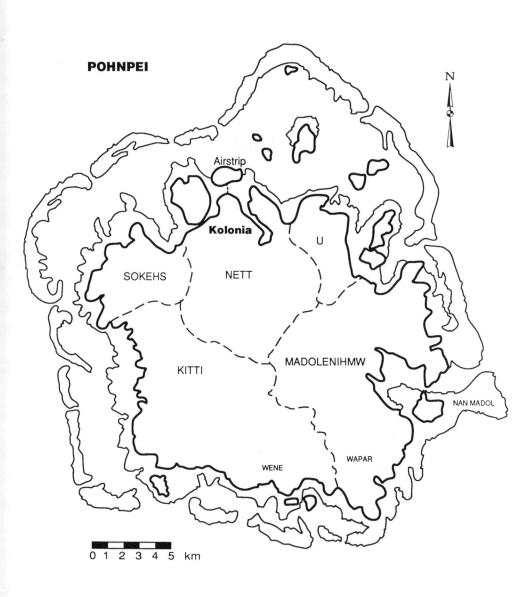

POHNPEI

N

Airstrip

Kolonia

U

SOKEHS

NETT

KITTI

MADOLENIHMW

NAN MADOL

WENE

WAPAR

0 1 2 3 4 5 km

Once Upon a Time

This is a tale about adventures of an anthropologist living on an island in Micronesia. The story is about quarter-ton yams, sex, sorcery, tin shacks, feasts, heart disease, babies, and a drink called kava. While I have included my experiences of being lost on the lagoon, eating dog, getting pregnant, and hiking mountain trails, the real adventures are surviving in a different culture, learning a new language, adjusting to strange customs, making friends, losing friends, and doing research.

Many people have fantasies in the traditions of the painter Paul Gauguin and the writer James Michener about bare-breasted maidens, pristine beaches, and waving palms in the South Pacific. Most do not know about the vast ocean area of Micronesia in the northern Pacific above the equator. Micronesia means "tiny islands" and is a scattering of land with a combined area no larger than Rhode Island stretching between Hawaii and the Philippines (see map). The United States has administered these chains of tropical islands as a Trust Territory from the United Nations since the end of World War II. Many Americans know about Guam, which was discovered by Ferdinand Magellan and has been the site of U.S. military bases since the United States acquired the island from Spain in 1898. But the 2,141 tiny islands covering three million square miles, an area as large as the continental United States, have been largely undiscovered in popular consciousness.

Pohnpei, in the center of Micronesia, is a high island forged millenia ago by volcanic action. It is about equidistant in nautical miles between the cities of Honolulu and Manila. The main island, which even now reveals its volcanic ancestry, has a roughly pentagonal shape and a maximum diameter of thirteen miles. A fringing coral reef encircles the volcanic core, forming a loose protection

1

and a line between lagoon and the open ocean beyond. Within the lagoon, the coral bottom is a world of rare beauty only divers can appreciate. There are low coral islets with sandy beaches in the lagoon, but the main island is largely surrounded by dense mangrove swamps that provide wood, food, and protection from erosion. Because of the swamps, the island fails to correspond to idealized notions of Pacific Islands. Visitors are surprised to see so few beaches, yet awestruck by the towering cliffs of Sokehs Island, the mountain forests, the dramatic colors of the vegetation, and the textures of tropical life. Pohnpei is justifiably regarded as one of most beautiful islands in the Pacific.

It rains most of the time. More than 200 inches a year fall on the lowlands and the uninhabited mountain center receives about 400 inches. In a sense, the island creates its own rain system by collecting the clouds as they pass. There are few cloudless days, which is all to the good since the heat can be intense. The rain creates both incredible humidity and magnificent waterfalls tumbling down basaltic cliffs. Rivers of clean, cool water run from the interior and in them people bathe, swim, and wash clothing.

I moved to this lovely island as part of a medical research team in the early 1970s. It was the fulfillment of a dream about doing fieldwork that I had harbored since high school. The core of our research team consisted of three anthropologists. The senior member was Dr. John (Jack) Fischer, who had worked in Micronesia when the United States Navy inherited it from the Japanese after World War II. He spoke Japanese, Trukese, and Pohnpeian. Because of the years he and his wife, Ann, spent there, his linguistic fluency, and his respect for the Pohnpeians' customs, he was something of a cult hero. Jack was also a former Marine, had three degrees from Harvard University, was a professor at Tulane University, published extensively, and had been District Anthropologist in Pohnpei when its name was spelled Ponape. During the research team's first summer there, his job was to develop contacts, establish the project, and lend his credibility to its success.

My husband, Roger, was a graduate student doing dissertation research. He wanted to study traditional medical systems and the diagnosis and curing of disease as Pohnpeians viewed it. Among other jobs, he served as budget director and motor scooter mechanic. Later our focus broadened to include such topics as sex, sorcery, incest, and politics.

I had already done fieldwork in the United States and completed my degree. When the grant was approved for this project, I took a research leave from my teaching post at a university in New Orleans. My job in the field was hiring, training, and supervising interviewers to administer the census, sample, and questionnaires. Somehow, baking cakes was also included. Roger and I had to learn the language quickly in order to manage the entire field portion of the project through to the completion of the medical examinations. Other members of the professional team, including a cardiologist, a psychologist, an epidemiologist, and several nurse-administrators, joined us for brief periods.

We had a large grant from the National Institute of Health to study the complex relations between social change, modernization and the high blood pressure that leads to heart attacks. The Pohnpei project had been started at the University of North Carolina School of Public Health by a group of dedicated professionals lead by Dr. John Cassel, well-known in the fields of public health, cardiology, and medical anthropology for his research on high blood pressure. Most Westerners know about the dangers of heart attacks for themselves and others; we know about blood pressure rising with age. Researchers believed that life-style, heredity, and many factors in the way Westerners lived or thought or felt influenced their health. But many areas of this puzzle remained unclear and even disputed. Several field studies such as ours had been started. Other studies that took blood pressures and did physical exams had been conducted in many locations, including the South Pacific.

To make a complicated theoretical and statistical issue simpler, we had looked for an island to provide science with a natural experiment. Water provides the boundaries that artificial borders do not. We wanted to test some theories about the cultural, social, and psychological determiners of blood pressure and heart disease. Studies done in societies which are changing rapidly, urbanizing and industrializing, generally showed higher blood pressure levels that rise with age. In smaller, less stressed societies that are not so exposed to radically new life styles, blood pressure does not rise with age and heart disease is absent or rare.

But this is not a book about science or blood pressure. The research project was the reason I was there and explains why at some moment I happened to be arguing about a pig, asleep in a feast house, or carrying sugar cane stalks over one shoulder. This is a personal encounter with team research, strange customs, an awkward environment, and my own personality.

When I first heard about the island through required readings in graduate school, it was called Ponape (*pon-a-pay*). In the scientific literature, on many maps, and in one corner of my mind, it will continue to be called that. However, changing political realities and a new sense of identity have led to a new spelling in western alphabets for what the residents themselves call their home. Now the island is officially named Pohnpei (*pone-pay*). The people and the language they speak are called Pohnpeian.

With a writer's privilege, I have collapsed and altered the timing of events to bring simplicity to concurrent happenings. I have probably imparted more wisdom to myself in recounting these events than I deserve. The written accounts, letters, field notes, and reports from this period have provided a framework, but memory and shifts in my own consciousness alter my perspectives.

I changed some personal names; the people of Pohnpei sometimes change their own names on important occasions. Some events and stories are omitted or disguised, because the participants are still alive. The only sin I have not knowingly committed is to distort the lives and customs of the people of this island. I want through mere words to convey my respect for the integrity of this culture. I am trusting that the people of Pohnpei will remember what they taught me and appreciate how much an understanding of their lives has to offer the rest of us.

I am deeply indebted to my friends and colleagues who have read this work and offered me their insights. This includes Dr. Glenn Petersen, Dr. Suzanne Falgout, Dr. Joseph Guillotte, Ann Edwards, June Powell, Eve Pinsker, and Dr. Michael Lieber. Pohnpei is uniquely blessed or cursed with an extraordinary compliment of field workers who have enriched our understanding of anthropology beyond measure. We owe tribute to the founding generation of giants: Saul Riesenberg, John Fischer, Ann Fischer, William Bascom, Daniel Hughes, and the other greats of Micronesian anthropology whose students we are. Anthropology is a craft practiced and passed on like family traditions or genes. Now, we have descendants who follow the customs, go into the field with fresh perspectives, and return to enlarge our discipline.

I have included a list of books and articles on Pohnpei. This is to honor those who have slogged through mud, verbs, and kinship systems and to assure you that this tale is only one view of a very complex society and a very complicated subject. All of us who have worked on Pohnpei have a special fellowship, even as, among ourselves, we argue over interpretations, mourn our dead, gossip furiously, and still smell coconut husk fires on a humid morning. We have long ago, among ourselves, accepted that no one person can fully explain an island culture as dynamic as Pohnpei.

The illustrations that grace this book are the work of Nancy Zoder Dawes, whose lines and pens and paper capture another spirit of truth. I am deeply grateful for the insights her artistry gives me. Printech of New Orleans produced the computer graphics for the maps. I would particularly like to thank Tom Curtin at Waveland Press for his belief in humanistic and creative anthropology.

This book was not written for my peers or professional colleagues. It is only what John van Maanen calls "an impressionist tale" (1988:101). The luminous work of the impressionist painters "sets out to capture a worldly scene in a special instant or moment of time. The work is figurative, although it conveys a highly personalized perspective. What a painter sees, given an apparent position in time and space, is what the viewer sees." As in those paintings I admire so much, I wish to evoke images, a sense of immediacy, and the feeling that you are there participating and observing. I believe that the events and feelings and people described here are universal and timeless. They are not unique to Pohnpei of the 1970s, but happen in many human cultures and happen to many others — not just anthropologists. I have only hinted at the realities between the dots of the painting and make no effort to analyze each dot in the painting. This is not an ethnography or history. This is only a true story about the doing of fieldwork and the doing of anthropology. It is written for those who are curious about other people's lives, or who may have wished, from time to time, to live on a tropical island and to be an anthropologist.

- 1 -

Fruit in the Hands
of the Gods

Once upon a time, a man named Sapkini built a large canoe. He believed that such a canoe could sail far away and find land. He knew that the sky is a roof and that it touches the sea at its edges. Where the sky meets the sea, his people would find land. They sailed with the hopes of a good land. On the way, they met an octopus. "I am Litakiti and I live in a shallow place in the water that flows from north to south." In the place the octopus had described was a reef. A small piece of coral rose above the reef, so small that it fit between the canoe and its outrigger.

The people brought rocks and stones from faraway lands. But the waves broke up the stones. So they planted mangrove trees to protect the island. But still the ocean was too close. So they decided to build a fringing reef around the island. Two women brought soil and the island grew larger. On the top the people made an altar. So the name of this new land was called *Pohn-Pei,* Upon-the-Altar.

The feast house of the High Chief of Nett was quiet. Men and women sat cross-legged on raised platforms along the three sides below the thatched roof. The fourth side was open to a view of stars in a clear sky. On the rocky ground between the platforms rested large flat stones. The men seated beside the stones removed their shirts and women placed flower wreaths in everyone's hair and rubbed scented coconut oil on their bare backs.

At a signal, the men began to pound the broken roots and twigs heaped on the stones in front of them. The rocks they held in their hands made deep ringing sounds as they struck. When the roots and twigs were broken down by the pounding, the men spread them with slow and practiced gestures into a long bundle of fibers.

7

One of the men picked up the two ends of the bundle and began to twist it, much as a wet towel is wrung. With gentle strength he continued to coil the bundle against itself until a thick brown liquid oozed out. Another man caught the flow with a round bottomed coconut cup. Rising to his feet, this man approached the High Chief, seated on the woven mats at the head of the U-shaped feast house. Averting his gaze, he extended the cup across his bent forearm, offering it to his Chief who drank the viscous liquid.

Later, as turns came around, I had my first taste of kava. It was astringent and slimy. It tasted like all the strong roots our ancestors used for medicine had been mixed together and looked like strings of swarthy mucus. The first sip numbed my lips, tongue, and throat. I surreptitiously picked out pieces of woody debris from my teeth.

Understanding none of the speeches, I enjoyed the feel of coconut oil on my arms, the smell of fresh flowers in my hair, and the shadows cast by the light of kerosene lanterns. I was fascinated by the serenity of the gestures, each of which seemed to carry an ancient tradition. Of course, I had read of the pepper plant whose roots were pounded on basaltic stones selected for their acoustic properties, and I knew that the communal drinking of kava is the heart of ceremonial life, much as communion is for Christians. I had heard that sipping too much would induce sleepiness but never intoxication as I thought of it. I had yet to understand that the preparation of kava has the power to promote communal harmony and peaceful social relationships. I had yet to need its healing powers.

One of the men moved over next to Jack, Roger and me and began to tell the story about the octopus and the reef. Another man translated it into English. I took notes as a good anthropologist should. Here, after all, was a genuine origin myth recounted by genuine natives. I had not asked the questions to which he was clearly giving me the answers. As the kava cup circulated again through the prescribed ritual sequences, I felt overwhelmed by the enormity of learning, then understanding, and then communicating the ancient meanings of this culture. I was inundated with sensations and information.

Later, we adjourned to a western-style house for a buffet. The tables were laden with dishes featuring breadfruit, taro, and yams cooked in different ways, some dishes seasoned with coconut milk or mashed bananas. The pork had been cooked in soy sauce. Some of the younger men spoke excellent English and, as I later learned, had degrees from American universities. The conversation revolved around development prospects for the island (a perennial topic). They discussed the pros and cons of the nascent tourist boom, the hope for a Pohnpeian-owned fishing industry, and the excitement surrounding the newly inaugurated Continental Air Micronesia Airlines jet flight to the islands. The men gossiped about Trust Territory politics and recent High Court decisions.

The evening was marked by the contrast between traditions older than any in my own brash, young culture and the pseudosophistication of modernization. It was my first glimpse into the vitality of the Pohnpeians' customs and their struggles with the forces of a world beyond their control. I tried to reconcile the glamor of doing fieldwork on an island of extraordinary tropical beauty with the realities of life in a colonial Third World island.

Only a week before, Jack Fischer had met me and my husband, Roger, at what was fondly called an airport. The landing of a 727 jet on the small islet in the lagoon was still a novelty to the Pohnpeians. Seaplanes had occasionally landed in the lagoon before a bare coral landing strip was built through a flattened mangrove swamp running between the watery ends of the islet. There were no lights, no tower, no radio contact between plane and ground, and no ground services of any kind. Once the strip was built, the two Continental jets, each carrying a mechanic and spare parts managed to land in Pohnpei three times a week when the weather was favorable. The new airport was a new two-room, traditional-style building of bamboo and thatch. As the 727 banked to land, the passengers could see a stunning rock formation called the Sokehs cliffs towering over the bays and lagoons.

My first sight of Kolonia, the capital of Pohnpei, was not favorable. This shanty town was supposed to be an example of urbanization, ethnic diversity, and development. It was home for most of the outislanders—those who come from other islands of Micronesia—and the foreigners, mostly a handful of Americans in the Trust Territory government. My first impression was one of overwhelming vegetation: breadfruit, palms, bananas, hibiscus, taro, lime, mango, bamboo, coconut, and hundreds of others I could not name. Weeds and mildew grew everywhere else. Rampant vegetation concealed the density of population. Many houses were built off the road where trees and terrain obscured their presence. The few miles of unpaved roads were dusty in the dry spells and muddy after rains.

My second impression was not only of the primitiveness that permeated the town, but also the feeling of civilization gone berserk. Huge piles of rusting, rotting trash stood outside the new airport building and the headquarters of the district administration. Women drew water from outdoor spigots while abandoned cars rusted nearby. Newer cars that had not yet succumbed to the hardships of the tropics were parked wherever they had stopped.

The stores and businesses had no signs because local people knew their names. The town had a Protestant church, a Catholic mission, the ruins of a Spanish fort, the district hospital, administrative offices, several good restaurants, and nineteen bars. But there were no zoning laws, building codes, city planning, or attempts to build an urban life. Everything was haphazard, temporary, jerry-rigged. The tropics are a great equalizer, and even new construction had begun to rot and age quickly. Cheap materials, such as tin and cinder block, were ubiquitous. In the incessant rain, they rusted in earth tones of reds, ochres and browns.

In the midst of this urban disorder, Jack had found for a home an appalling shack on a side road leading from Kolonia's main street. The roof of the lean-to kitchen had collapsed. The walls came only halfway up to the rusty tin roof. The only door had to be lifted into place. Mosquitos, flies, geckos, lizards, mice, and—to my special horror—rats were the shanty's main tenants. He was unjustifiably proud of the dump that was to be his home for three months. Roger was unnerved by the thought of sleeping on the floor, animals or no, while I was disgusted by the thought of having to follow the custom of removing my shoes to enter. To placate me, Jack generously agreed to refer to the rats as ground squirrels and to run an illegal electrical line from the jail on the hill into the shanty so there could be a light.

Jack needed his hovel for the visits of two other researchers, Floyd and Ian, so he arranged for Roger and me to live temporarily in a real house usually occupied by a Peace Corps administrator. My senses had not yet acculturated, so I judged this house only by western standards and took for granted its amenities of appliances, electricity, beds, indoor plumbing, and a kitchen sink. But it was a hard house in which to live. I still adhered unconsciously to the standards of housekeeping learned at my mother's knee. Termites had eaten away everything but the paint, and the house was sifting slowly into dust. We shook our sheets free of termite dust in the morning and again at night. I did time-consuming housekeeping chores that Jack could ignore in his shack.

The house, so indisputably western, isolated us and did not lure the Pohnpeians into an easy rapport. The furniture included tables, chairs, couches, beds, and desks. The kitchen had counter space and cabinets. Later, when I lived very differently, I realized how alien waist-high living was to a Micronesian woman whose household life is spent on the floor. Furthermore, the yard was landscaped as only those descended from European cultures see space. There was a sidewalk with flowers on each side, as well as a front yard and a back yard.

Awkward though it was, the house gave us breathing space to adjust to these novel circumstances. We were fated to suffer culture shock. Anthropologists, travelers, or others cut off from the daily comfort of their own culture and language eventually react in strange ways. They may lose their tempers or retreat into alcohol, prejudice, or a dozen forms of escapism. Immersion in another culture is a shock. Simple things we take absolutely for granted — the taste of food, how to sit and stand, or words for yes and no — are gone. I understood cultural relativity from an intellectual perspective, but the gut reality feels very different. For example, all my senses tell me that the British drive on the wrong side of the road. Intellectually, I know that this is merely a minor cultural choice, a variation of possibilities, and no more God-given than the "right" side of the road we in the United States have chosen. But I still get angry at the British for being so pigheaded.

An objective observer or therapist would have recognized the forms our culture shock was taking. Roger wrote postcards to about 200 people to whom we had not even sent Christmas cards. He also lurked behind trees trying to take pictures of exposed maidenly breasts and he ordered useless items to be sent from his hometown. He says that these were perfectly normal behaviors under the circumstances and that I am the one who did weird things. It is true that I read ten-year-old magazines — even *Boys' Life* — and trashy novels from cover to cover (when I could find any). I also made up lists like this:

—hire interviewers
—eat mango for breakfast
—learn to speak Pohnpeian
—find that bobby pin

I posted lists and cleaned house more than necessary for someone who had cheerfully given up material goods and the American mania for possessions.

Jack had his own ideas of what we needed to learn. He taught me how to fill, clean and cook on a smelly kerosene camp stove and graciously ate the raw or burned results. As he demonstrated the proper way to trim the wick, he lectured us on linguistics or folklore.

"Somewhere there is a sound like 'h.' It may be very important. Write down all the occurrences you hear." (I never heard any.)

"Here are some questions you will need: How is this thing like that thing? How is this thing different from that thing?" (This represented a level of sophistication that I could not have hoped to reach in months, perhaps years, assuming I was interested.)

"Listen for stories about eating forbidden animals or horned fish or twins or sibling rivalry." (I could barely say hello.)

Our first challenge—other than the oppressive heat, transportation, housing, adjustment, and learning the language—was to set up the research project.

The United States Navy had done a health survey in 1946, when it first started administering the island after the defeat of the Japanese in World War II. This survey revealed consistently low blood pressures and no apparent rise as people grew older. But the Navy doctors had only lined up a bunch of people and took their readings. We had very sophisticated hypotheses and needed to act scientifically if the data were to help with the dilemmas of heart disease.

We wrote the grant application for this project in the language of western science. Our goals claimed:

> to investigate the dependent variable, possible cardiovascular disease as manifested by high blood pressure, and the independent variable, individual response to social stress and change as related to personality types, degree of modernization, and the sense of belonging to organized groups in the social structure.

But the sickness "heart disease" does not even exist in traditional Pohnpeian medicine. Spirit sickness, yes; heart attacks, no. It is Westerners who believe that high blood pressure is the silent killer. To complicate matters further, the term for "blood pressure," much less words for "variable" or "hypothesis," do not exist in their Pohnpeian language.

We had to explain the research in ways that the Pohnpeians could understand. One of the first ways we used was a radio broadcast in which the director of the District Hospital read an explanation of the projects, translated here into English:

The movement of blood through the body can be strong or weak. The strong rather than the weak movement of the blood through the body can be caused by age, weight, diet, smoking, too much salt, lack of exercise, pregnancy, and some diseases. Strong movement taxes the heart and eventually causes sickness and death. This is happening increasingly in America and in countries whose life-styles are like that of Americans. A physical examination can reveal the strong movement of blood in a person's body.

However, this important disease is also related to worries and feelings that people have about their responsibilities, opportunities, and the swift changes occurring in Pohnpei. Being overworked, burdened with heavy responsibilities, or simply worried is not enough to cause this strong movement of blood we call high blood pressure. All of these feelings occurred among your ancestors in Pohnpei without a rise in blood pressure or similar sicknesses.

We conclude that not all Pohnpeians are prepared for the demands of a modern Micronesian nation, business, schools, economic and community development and new social problems. This is why the first interview asks for your feelings about change: "Would you rather your children learn about the time-honored traditions of Pohnpei or learn modern customs brought by the Americans?" You will be asked about your feelings of belonging: "Who would you turn to in times of trouble? What type of organizations do you belong to?" Other feelings that you have are also important: "Do you mind having your work interrupted? Are you impatient about having to wait?"

The broadcast also answered other questions: who was sponsoring this research, why some people were included and others were not; why healthy and sick people were included together; what the benefits were for Pohnpei and those who participated? We visited every official in the traditional system of government and in the American administration. We enlisted the support of the many Peace Corps volunteers whom the islanders trusted, and we established a base of operation with the cooperative personnel at the island's rudimentary hospital.

All the computers, copying machines, electric typewriters, and other staples of research were in North Carolina. For any practical purpose, there was not a telegraph or telephone system on the island. Few written records existed for the population of about 17,000. There were no house or telephone directories, social security or precinct registrations, or censuses, and few marriage licenses, birth certificates, land deeds, or other statistics for us to use. On the mountainous island, people shifted residences and changed their names quite frequently. So the research team would have to conduct our own census of the areas we had selected for sampling.

Pohnpei is divided into five districts shaped like pieces of a pie. Cut up in this fashion, each district includes high mountains, forests, coastal plains, shoreline, and lagoon. The five districts, called Madolenihmw, U, Nett, Kitti, and Sokehs, also have distinctive personalities. Each tells its own stories about wars, rebellions, boundary changes, unique events, and histories of succession to chiefly ranks. Each one has reasons to believe itself special and to compete with other districts. In the olden days, the men of the districts went to war against each other. Today, the competition centers on less bloody encounters.

Before we left the United States for Pohnpei, the team members agreed to concentrate on three areas of the island. We believed that modernization and the stresses of change would affect these parts differently. The first zone, the town of Kolonia, we too optimistically labeled urban. With a shifting population of about 3,000, it was the symbol of the massive changes affecting Pohnpeian society, many of which had been introduced by the American administration. The second zone, in the district of U, was near enough to Kolonia for commuting to school or work, but far enough away to make traditional ways of living off the land possible. The third zone, the rural area, was indeed remote. Wene, in the district of Kitti, was on the opposite side of the island from Kolonia and could only be reached by boat in a trip of three to six hours, depending on the tides. The residents of Wene prided themselves on preserving classical traditions better than their friends and relatives in the other areas had. But the price of cultural preservation was economic isolation. They had little chance to make money in this rural region. We imagined that the residents of the urbanizing Kolonia would feel the stresses of change and modernization more than the people living closer to Pohnpei's past.

The first step was to be a census of all the households in the three areas. While we were doing that, we were also writing and pretesting the long questionnaire that asked about the social, cultural, and psychological features related to blood pressure. While these questionnaires were printed and sent from North Carolina, we planned to train interviewers to administer them. In the final stage, a medical team from New Zealand and Australia would give thorough physical examinations to the more than 1,200 Pohnpeians in the sample. The results of the medical exams would be correlated with our anthropological findings, the census, and the questionnaires.

I had sworn to myself that I would avoid politics, either Micronesian or American. I wanted to study language, social organization, how children are reared, anything but political anthropology. I planned to resist the lure of the Paramount Chiefs, the machinations to high office, and the gossip about the U.S. politicians who controlled the destiny of Micronesia. I was paid to do research on blood pressure. But we needed a great deal of background information about people's feelings and the pressures on them. And what people wanted to talk about was politics. Every conversation either centered on or returned repeatedly to some form of politics. Finally I capitulated. I later came to appreciate and even to participate in political maneuvering.

In fact, the most important key to understanding this culture turned out to be the pervasive traditional political system. I could no more have avoided this reality than I could have ignored the breadfruit trees. From the first sip of kava in the feast house of the Paramount Chief of Nett, I was hooked into the political systems. From the first glimpse of traditional culture and the problems below the surface of a tropical paradise, I was drawn into currents and countercurrents I still strive to understand.

The polity of Pohnpei is complex and intricate. Each of the five districts or kingdoms has a system of rank or status that might be translated as hereditary nobility, landed gentry, and commoners. Each district is headed by a man called the Nahnmwarki, sometimes translated as king, but more accurately as Paramount Chief or High Chief. Below him are ranged some dozen high-titled nobles and priests in what might be called the A line. As a complement to this, there is a B line headed by another chief called the Nahnken, or "talking chief," and a set of nobles in that line. Anthropologists owe our colleague, Saul Riesenberg, for his painstaking descriptions of the intricacies of Pohnpeian polity and the terms for these lines.

It was neither the time nor the place to be proud of being an American. My naive patriotism was already severely tested by the Vietnam War. I had arrived on the island only weeks after the Kent State University killings and, as a college professor, had been embroiled in the protests sweeping over U.S. universities. I had looked forward to escaping from the political strife and materialism of U.S. culture. But it proved impossible to avoid the impact of U.S. foreign policy. I witnessed the most corrosive aspects of the Trusteeship government and my country's colonial control of what was only superficially an island paradise. We were continually questioned about the United State's involvement in the Southeast Asian war and the implications of the negotiations with the United States over independence for Micronesia.

Other than the official visits on behalf of the research project, I had little contact with the U.S. officials who were assigned to the Trust Territory administration on the island. They lived in lovely houses in a separate valley and rarely mixed with anyone else. The Peace Corps volunteers, on the other hand, spoke the language and had converted to a partisan view of Micronesian politics. Occasionally that summer, the research team ate at the local restaurants, the best of which was Stewo's. This was the gathering spot for Americans, Micronesians, and interesting visitors, and a good place to meet and exchange gossip. The chief topic of conversation throughout the time I lived there was the political activities of the United States government and the outcome and repercussions of the negotiations about the future status of Micronesia and of Pohnpei in particular. Tied to the issue of the political future of the islands was economic development: How can the islanders earn a living? Where is the money going to come from?

It was a benign form of colonialism. There were no beatings, political imprisonment, or even minor violations of human rights. In 1947, the United Nations had given political and military control of Micronesia (except for Guam, which it already possessed) to the United States. Japan, in losing the war, had lost this colonial empire and America was enjoined by the United Nations to exercise all due speed in moving this protected area into independence or some form of self-government with cooperative ties to the United States.

Until the 1960s, the U.S. government had ignored the farflung islands. But their strategic position along the eastern arc of Asia and the loss (or potential loss) of military positions in Japan, Okinawa, Southeast Asia, and the Philippines gave them new significance and ended decades of neglect. Other pressures from the United Nations to resolve their ambiguous territorial status steered what few policy makers in Washington who knew anything about the situation into a new plan of action. Budgets increased enormously and money for jobs poured into the Trust Territory.

This infusion of money in the absence of sensible development schemes created a systematic dependency upon U.S. money. To buy consumer goods in increasing amounts, more jobs were needed—even if the jobs were only make-work. This flood of money that was not a product of economic development also caused a severe generation gap between older men raised in the Japanese system, which emphasized respect for elders and strict obedience, and the younger ones with dreams of money and easy jobs.

Even with increased budgets and the creation of new (make-work) bureaucratic jobs, the basic tasks of colonial administration did not get done. Trash was not collected; sewer and water systems were either poorly maintained or not built. Very few of the basic structures needed for development were ever put in place by the U.S. administration. The development proclaimed by the United States was a myth, a chimera.

As one example, a number of Micronesians appeared on my job surveys as employees of the telephone system. But I never met anyone, except a few Americans, who had a telephone or had completed a call. Sometimes political appointees from the United States were dumped there; few stayed very long and even fewer learned the language or really talked with Micronesians.

I heard a lot of gossip at Stewo's restaurant about Central Intelligence Agency (CIA) agents operating in Micronesia, or about Department of Defense operatives, or about Americans posing as researchers to learn secrets about the Micronesians, or about officials bugging Micronesians' meetings, or about U.S. bureaucrats maneuvering to undermine the status talks. In fact, we were questioned rather closely until it became obvious that we were dressed too eccentrically to be spies. Real agents were said to have short hair, business suits, and no intention of learning the language.

Social science research has occasionally provided a convenient cover for spying or covert activities. Anthropologists at that time were going through a period of both painful self-criticism and active disassociation with government agencies such as the CIA and the Department of Defense, whose policies were seen as injurious to the native peoples we studied and whose trust we tried to earn. Important to this story, however, is the existence of the rumors, gossip, fears, and paranoia. I do not know the truth value of these, that is, who really did what, when, why, and for whom. The same viewpoint will also be true when I tell about sorcery.

Shopping for food was a constant challenge and learning the system absorbed much of my adjustment energy. Kolonia had nothing resembling a supermarket. There were a half-dozen small stores stocking very expensive imported goods. Next to the canned mackerel and corned beef, which were staples of our diet, were bolts of brightly colored Japanese cloth, hundred-pound sacks of rice, sugar, and flour, and imported canned soda pop. Only one store had refrigeration or freezer facilities. Another was owned by a family that had come from Belgium in the early part of the century and carried such unpredictable treasures as genuine Scottish oatmeal and a sheet of Formica. Ordinary objects we usually take for granted—batteries, film, and razor blades—had to be specially ordered.

All of the stores were dependent on ships from Japan, Australia, the United States, or European countries. If there was any organizing principle for ships' arrivals or cargo, I never discovered it. Beer and soft drinks always seemed to flow off the ships, but toilet paper was irregular. One ship brought only Ketchup. If I saw canned tomato sauce, I bought it; three weeks later, another ship might bring spaghetti noodles. If hamburger meat came in, spaghetti was possible. If not, I substituted canned corned beef.

Fresh produce should have been easily available in this lush tropical environment where plants grow easily. But the marketing system had many kinks in it. No one could predict what would be available at the small produce market from hour to hour. Fresh fish might be obtained about 5 o'clock in the afternoon at the dock where the boats tied up, if a boat had gone out and caught something. Although Japanese and U.S. fishing fleets caught hundreds of tons of fish only miles from the island, the fish was processed by modern technology thousands of miles away and only reached Pohnpei in expensive cans. Instead of fresh fish, the staple of our diet was canned mackerel. White rice, another daily fare, was also imported, although the island had supplied rice to the Japanese during World War II.

No one was in any danger of going hungry. The rich island ecology produced surpluses of nourishing food. But the Pohnpeians, like anyone else, had developed food preferences. They liked the ease and status of canned food. Amid the bounty of the ocean, they chose canned mackerel. From the Japanese, they had acquired a love of white rice, and from the Americans, sugar, salt, and white processed flour. American foods had high status because they were very expensive, but the desire for alcoholic drinks and imported canned foods also contributed to the dependency on the flow of U.S. money.

I fell in love with breadfruit. The tree on which this treasure grows is botanically related to the fig or mulberry. Broad, deep green, and serrated leaves filter the sunlight against trunk and branches, which are reminiscent of temperate-zone oaks. The fruit, which is gathered by children who climb the trees, is round like a beach ball. When the rough green peel is removed, a hard, ivory center is revealed. Breadfruit is one of the world's most nourishing and tasty carbohydrate foods. It is the reason why Captain Bligh was commissioned to sail his ship, the *Bounty*, to Tahiti and one of the reasons for the famous mutiny of Fletcher Christian.

I have eaten it boiled, baked, fried, dried in strips as candy, preserved in pits, and fermented. If allowed to ripen until soft and then baked, it tastes like the ultimate Fig Newton. Otherwise, the taste depends on the manner of preparation, but always delicious. It is no wonder that the Pohnpeians call it "fruit in the hands of the gods." It was difficult to appreciate rice and canned mackerel when breadfruit was free and in season.

Just as I was learning how to keep house in a strange culture, another member of our team arrived. Floyd took one look at Jack's dump, pronounced it a slum dwelling, and refused to enter it, much less to sleep on its floor. Declaring Jack's happy domesticity in the face of deplorable housing conditions to be simple madness, he moved in with us.

Floyd was a psychologist temporarily assigned to the project for his special abilities in writing a questionnaire that would tap the social and psychological dimensions that relate to high or low blood pressure. Floyd was a good husband, a good father, a good Christian, a good citizen of the United States, a good teacher, and a good psychologist. It was fascinating to work with him because he had an absolutist view of culture. Some things are right; some things are wrong.

Human behavior, he conceded, can be understood by looking at individuals' feelings and opinions. Cultural influences, belief systems, and customs might be interesting, but they did not explain why people behaved in a certain way. He had a naive belief that people anywhere in the world were predictable by their common humanity. Therefore, the concepts of western psychological sciences could be universally applied. He also believed that there were natural laws in the world that all people followed.

The first of his laws was that women naturally waited on men. The first week Floyd lived with us included many adjustments and, without much thought, I waited on him and provided some of the same domestic services my husband took for granted. I got breakfast, straightened up the house, cooked, and made the daily rounds of small stores. I had plenty of help from Jack, who had strong domestic skills and a wife who was a professional anthropologist. But after a week or so, Floyd brought me his laundry and asked when it would be finished. Although there was a washing machine in the Peace Corps house, it was broken, and I had been washing my personal things by hand. Without thinking, I fixed the machine and did the men's laundry. Such is the force of natural law.

I am ashamed to admit that I might have continued to wait on him, but for the fact that his dependency was interfering with my own work. It was the little assumptions and the small tasks that ate into my time and energy: coffee, toast, and the constant patronage. He could not apologize for the messes he made because he just naturally made them, and he could not be expected to cook because only wives knew how. He communicated with me only about what he considered my real work, which was managing our little household. Despite the equivalence of our degrees and titles, he could not accept me as an equal partner on the research project.

One night at supper, my patience finally snapped. We were discussing a party for key Americans in Kolonia. It was obvious that I was going to do the work and he was going to receive the credit. In my first act of feminist rebellion, I wrote down all the jobs connected to domestic management as well as to the party. After each job, I wrote the name of one of the four of us. Then I angrily posted the duty roster on the termite-ridden wall. Jack just winked. He was accustomed to the same system in his household. Floyd was aghast. He fumed, then reasoned, then resorted to natural law. He was a professional, he was sent to do an important job, his wife treated him with proper respect, and so forth. He tried unsuccessfully to convince Roger to bring his wife in line. But I was deeply angry at having two full-time jobs when the men each had only one. I am only sorry that I did not discover assertiveness sooner.

Our conflicts about gender, professionalism, and the division of labor were quite apart from Floyd's misgivings about anthropologists and the concept of cultural relativity we practiced. The questionnaire we were writing together included an important section on clan membership. Everyone on Pohnpei, as in many traditional societies, is very conscious of clan membership. It determines marriage choices to some extent, since it would be incest for Pohnpeians to marry someone of the same clan. Titles and social status are handed down through the clans. Being born into or marrying into a prestigous clan is a route of social advancement.

But, like kinship systems in many other world societies, the Pohnpeian clans are matrilineal. That is, clan membership is reckoned through the female line. All Pohnpeians, male and female, acquire their clan status from their mother who got it from her mother and so on back to a mythical ancestress. This means that men cannot pass on clan membership to their sons or daughters. In fact, the most influential male in a clan would likely be a mother's brother.

Floyd was horrified. He denied the possibility of such severe social deviance. He did not hear matrilineal. He heard matriarchal. He was certain that we were saying women were in control and were the dominant sex, clearly a violation of natural law. He had absolutely never questioned the western practice of wives and children taking on their husband's and father's name and status. He was appalled when I pointed out how reasonable a custom matrilineal descent is in light of the fact that people can always be certain who their mother is but never certain who their father is. Furthermore, in matrilineal societies, children automatically take their mother's name and inherit from them, so illegitimacy as Westerners understand it does not occur. Despite its logic, matrilineal kinship struck at the center of Floyd's moral code.

We spent many happy hours debating cultural relativity and matrilineal clans. We debated religion, too. Floyd believed that the disciples of Jesus truly had seen Jesus returned from the dead, but that Micronesians who claimed to have witnessed ghosts on the path, or heard the spirits of departed relatives had only superstitions and a strong delusional structure. Every time I teach these concepts in an introductory anthropology class, I think of Floyd. I am not certain that we ever convinced him that just as people choose to trace descent through the father's line (as in western patrilineal history), they can equally choose the mother's line. I did succeed in keeping those questions as part of our research.

When we designed the budget for the grant and wrote the questionnaire, we assumed that we could hire bilingual young men as interviewers, the local equivalent of college students who do that work for minimum wages in the United States. My first hirings were disasters. One of the fellows ran off with the typewriter. Another giggled and looked shyly at his toes when we mentioned the questionnaire. A third had ambitions for status and money which outran his abilities. None of them had what either Westerners or Pohnpeians consider good work habits.

They were paralyzed by their lack of standing in a society that values the wisdom of age. As I slowly discovered, males in Pohnpei stay youths and are not accorded adult status until they reach their forties. With age come the high titles by which respect is measured. A youngster with no significant title does not ask highranking or older people personal questions. Nor will he be listened to when he speaks in public places. A job cannot be very important if callow youths are sent to do it. This left us rather in a bind: where were we going to find interviewers?

One evening shortly after Floyd's merciful departure, we had just finished a rare dinner of sweet and sour pork when a visitor arrived. He was dressed in dark trousers, a shortsleeved white shirt and a navy blue baseball cap. I greeted him with my very limited command of Pohnpeian, but Jack conducted the conversation.

Together, we walked down a hill to his house. Jack wanted to check out some notebooks that this man had written. A few of the adult men keep diaries, records, or written accounts. Since little of Pohnpeian life is written down and the men are so reticent about giving out certain kinds of information, Jack always watched for these documents. He had made some fascinating finds, such as the Luellen Bernart documents on which he was working for publication. In this case, the notebooks proved to be of less value than the man's writing skills. Although he spoke no English, he was literate in Japanese and, rare for a Pohnpeian, knew one of the conflicting orthographies or scripts for writing his language.

Sohn Alpet (John Albert in English) was at that time in his middle sixties. He had a socially prominent or high title in the A line of the district of Madolenihmw. He had been conscripted by the Japanese Army and sent to fight in New Guinea. Of his group of conscripts, he was the only one to return and was, therefore, one of Pohnpei's celebrated war heroes. When I knew him better, he confided two main impressions of those years. First, kava was growing but no one prepared or drank it. Second, Japanese troops along with native troops had to practice cannibalism during the harsh conditions of the war. Sohn Alpet was a devout family man and an elder in the Protestant church.

Jack was impressed with Sohn Alpet and urged us to hire him. I was leery. The man spoke no English and, as far as I could tell, knew nothing about the conduct of social science research. He had never worked with Americans or held a regular job. Roger and I discussed this exhaustively as we continued to look for our ideal college student. Meanwhile, Jack quietly eased Sohn Alpet into the job.

Sohn Alpet began to take his tasks very seriously. He started to carry a black plastic briefcase and within two weeks showed up for work with his own assistant. From within his kinship network he had hired himself an obedient youth, Roswel, whom he intended to use as interpreter and secretary. Sohn Alpet supervised his assistant and we paid him, an unorthodox but successful solution.

Hiring Sohn Alpet was, as it turned out, a stroke of serendipity in research. In time he became an interpreter of Pohnpeian life, an interpreter even about life itself. Anthropologists usually call such assistants "informants." But the term sounds like a character in a spy novel to the uninitiated. I prefer the word "friend" or "teacher." Today, we would use the title consultant in the truest sense of the word.

Although Jack's knowledge and understanding had eased Roger and me over many hard times, I was still trying to establish a western domesticity, conduct a research project, and adjust to dirt, noise, strange sensations, and different expectations.

Learning the language quickly and well was crucial. But imagine the process of learning a language where there are no dictionaries, grammars, classes, or teacher's help. Fortunately, the Peace Corps had produced a small mimeographed introduction to Pohnpeian that used an easy method. First, we learned a few fixed phrases:

> Hello, goodbye
> Yes, no, right, wrong, excuse me
> Thank you, please
> My name is _____. What is your name?
> What is this called in Pohnpeian? How do you say this?
> Where is _____?

We collected nouns. "What is the name for this?" Body parts, objects in nature such as trees, flowers, sun, moon and stars; names of buildings; terms for relatives; types of machines; doors and roof; roads, rocks, and fish. With a growing number of nouns, adjectives were added: colors, quantities (how many), qualities (good, bad, big, little), and descriptions. Soon it was possible to make short sentences based on simple patterns:

> the fish, the red fish
> the small red fish, two small red fishes
> The fish is red. The fish is small.
> Here is the fish. There is the fish. Where is the fish?
> The fish is not red. This is not a fish.

Substitute other nouns, numbers, colors or qualities and the number of sentences that can be produced increases exponentially.

The sounds of Pohnpeian are easy. The one that gives English speakers trouble is a consonant "t," for which there is no English equivalent. For us, the resulting sound is more like a "ch." We have a nasal sound at the end of such words as sing or ring. Pohnpeians have the same sound, but it is also used at the beginning of words. Dogs bark—*ngong,* bite—*ngalis,* and cast shadows—*ngehn.* A little practice provides mastery.

At first some words sounded just like other words but were obviously different to native speakers. The difference in meaning comes from the length of the vowel sound, whether it was long or short. So, *ma* means "if" and *mah* means "old," "aged," or "ripe." The added *h* is a writing symbol signifying that in speech the vowel is held longer, like maa. *Man* is an intransitive verb meaning "to take hold or be effective." *Mahn,* with a slightly longer vowel, is an animal or insect. Although we do not have such distinctions in English, it proved easy to hear and learn.

Sometimes scholars have claimed that the deepest meanings a culture holds about itself are imbedded in the structure of its language. For example, English emphasizes time—past, present, future, and subtle permutations of each. Its precision about tenses is said to contribute to the scientific mentality that marks English-speaking culture. If this theory is correct, then pronouns in the Pohnpeians' language reveal some important features of their world view.

They have an additional category of pronouns which came to make such sense to me that I still think "in the dual." English speakers say "they" meaning any group of two or more that does not include the speaker. Pohnpeians say one "they" for a general group of three or more and another "they" for just two things or people. The same is true for "you": there is "you" (singular), "you all" (plural), and "the two of you" or "you two" (the dual). English speakers just say, "We are going swimming." Pohnpeian speakers say, "We [all of us including you] are going swimming." Or, "We [exclusive of the persons being addressed, that is, not including you] are going swimming." Or, "We [just the two of us] are going swimming."

Possessive pronouns operate the same way. "Our boat" is a bit vague in English because the person we are speaking to may not be a partner in the boat. In Pohnpeian, "our boat" has two forms, one if everybody owns the boat and one for speaking to others about a boat in which they do not share ownership. At first I thought this sounded selfish. Later I appreciated the precision it permitted, and I have missed these forms in English.

But pronouns have one more striking feature. The words for "my, our, your, his, their" (indicating ownership) will change, depending on the noun. One form indicates ownership of personal things, such as clothes, parents, or spouses. A second category includes plants, animals, children, and small objects. If you discuss something to eat, you use another set of words and still another for something to drink. Forms of transportation, such as scooters, cars, canoes, or boats, require their special forms. Brothers and sisters have a different category, as do sacred objects. There are even more categories of nouns that require their own possessive forms, but these are the ones in daily use. Why in a culture in which cooperation and sharing are so emphasized would there be so many ways of showing possession? Or perhaps a better question, what impulses cause us to use language to divide up the real world into such arbitrary categories?

I have made this business of learning another language sound easy. I have omitted the frustration of the early stages when even dogs understood more than I did. Any three-year-old child did better on those simple sentences than I did. The subleties and innuendo I wanted to express (and could in English) were impossible. For months, I sweated profusely when I had to carry on a full conversation in Pohnpeian. It was no gentle perspiration, either; it was the sweat of hard, dirty work.

Nonetheless, I will never forget the elation of deciphering and using relative clauses or personal pronouns. Nor will I forget the agony of stepping on a woman's toes. Instead of asking forgiveness, I blurted out, "His canoe is blue."

To celebrate our progress in setting up the research project and the language study, and in making our first adjustments, Jack took us on a holiday trip to Nan Madol, the largest archaeological site in the Pacific Ocean. In the shallow lagoon between the island of Tewmen and the fringing reef, the ancestors of the Pohnpeians had, more than a thousand years before, built a walled city of canals, a tropical Venice covering nine square miles. More than one hundred artificial islands linked by canals were constructed out of polygonal basaltic crystals that look like Lincoln Logs. It is hard to believe that such regular forms occur in nature and perhaps harder to understand how people moved so many tons of stone from quarries high in the mountains to the lagoon floor. On some of the artificial islands, the walls of the citadels and fortresses are at least twenty feet high.

To build this stunning city, the ancient Pohnpeians used only rafts and simple tools, but they apparently had a genius for social organization. What inspired them to labor so long and hard to build the temple complexes through which only water traffic may pass? Ceremonial use of the site was abandoned in the nineteenth century when approximately half of the population died in a smallpox epidemic. But the awe that it must have inspired can still be felt. The contrast of this gracious planned city to the randomness and dirt of Kolonia was stunning.

A letter from the field:

Dearest Ones,

It is hot, hot, hot. We are sweltering. I feel mildewed all over. Yesterday, as on most days, it rained. All the leather stuff we brought has begun to rot, and there is a thickening layer of green goo over sandals, belts, camera case, and so forth. The aspirin tablets have disintegrated into a fine powder.

Everyone wears those rubber thongs you use for beach or showers at home. They are called *zories* because the Japanese introduced them. Also, the Japanese custom of removing your shoes before entering any house is followed here. You don't have to leave your zories outside churches, the hospital, government offices, or stores. But private residences have a stack outside, and it is just good manners to take yours off. I laugh about those signs in the USA against barefooted or bare-chested hippies.

Roger and I love our new Suzuki 70 motor scooter. For various reasons, the grant can't buy a Jeep or a boat. The motor scooter is much more practical. The 30-mile-per-hour speed limit on Main Street is just a dare. Only a foolish person would try to drive that fast. Some of the roads are so rocky and full of pot holes from incessant rains that the bike has to be pushed. Did you know that you can ride a motor scooter and carry an umbrella at the same time?

Last weekend we hiked up into the mountains of the district of Nett. We saw the ruins of the Japanese-built hydroelectric generating plant (sure beats the kerosene-fueled monster that provides intermittent electricity for Kolonia). Our destination was several lovely waterfalls at about 2,000 feet. Here the tropical rain forest vegetation is even more extraordinary than along the shore. Many trees and rocks were covered with a cushion of green moss. Kolonia seemed cool and sophisticated when we returned.

Jack's daughter, Mary Ann, born here when he was District Anthropologist in the 1950s, has just joined us. She has adjusted to the trash heap he lives in, although her slumber has been interrupted by peeping Toms, young boys who spy at the windows. Her peeper was a kid from the jail; security is lax, to say the least, and boys from there wander around at night. Jack reported this petty crime, but no one seems concerned. When she and I went up to the police station yesterday to register the motor scooter, we heard giggling and shuffling. Looking down through the wide cracks in the floor of the veranda, we saw a group of teenage boys peering up at us. American women are objects of great curiosity. Jack says that I should ignore the stares and ride the motor scooter astride rather than sidesaddle. He laughed and said that if we are seen together on the motor scooter, people will think we are having an affair.

Working with Jack is a constant delight. None of my anxieties of being in the field with such a famous anthropologist have materialized. It will be very difficult to follow in his footsteps. At a meeting with the hospital staff last week, he gave a long lecture on blood pressure and heart disease in Pohnpeian. He only had to ask for the Pohnpeian word for kidney. All of the senior people seem to know and respect him. Jack is the official fresh-food purchaser for our little group, a task he takes very seriously. Yesterday he returned with mangos, papayas, and a pineapple. He sniffed each carefully and laid them out on the windowsill. Then he announced that the mango would be ripe in time for supper, but that the papayas would be at their peak about 3:00 in the morning.

Mother, your lessons in baking did not cover a lemon cake mix with a coupon on the back that said you must redeem it before March 30, 1959. The cake mix was a strange gray color and I had to beat it with a hammer before I could add the eggs. Incidentally, eggs are scarce, and I got two only by following some chickens. It was Jack's birthday, and the cake was widely judged a success.

We eat out at least once a day. Organizing cooking while learning all these new foods and customs is too difficult to do three times a day. Anyway, it is a chance to meet people and to try new foods. I love the raw tuna fish with hot horseradish sauce and the bland local foods, such as breadfruit, taro, yams, and bananas of many varieties.

For amusement, we went to the movies the other night. You have to be a desperate moviegoer like Roger to appreciate the *Sports Highlights of 1949* and *Jason and the Argonauts*. We sat on backless wooden benches while the rain beat heavily on the old tin roof and kids and babies took over the floor. Usually the projector, the only one on the island, fails to perform or provides only the sound, only the picture, or bits of each. But it costs only a quarter, and the enthusiastic response and audience participation makes it all enjoyable.

Yes, you can send us something. How about 10 plastic coat hangers (the wire ones rust over everything) and an egg carton (one of those cardboard ones your eggs come from the store in). I can't buy a dozen eggs until I have something to carry them in on the motor scooter. Also, some germicidal soap like Phisohex because a bite or blister can so quickly become infected here and Americans have horrible tropical ulcers when they don't take care of their skin. Thank you for all the stuff you sent last week.

Kasehlehlia—that means goodbye (and hello) in Pohnpeian.

- 2 -

Green Leaves on Stories

Kava here is what the cross is to the Christian; it fell from heaven and is the only means of obtaining a hearing there . . . to these people kava is the only means of communication with their spirits; they hold a cup of this drink, always in their hands, when addressing the object of prayer.

—The missionary Sturgis, 1856

The sunrise was spectacular on the morning we began our trip to Wene. The air was filled with the sounds and smells unique to an island dawn. Jack had made arrangements for us to visit the remote community in the district of Kitti. We wanted to take a sample of about 300 people from this community on the opposite end of the island from Kolonia to represent the rural component in the project design. Ian, a cardiologist from New Zealand who would head the medical team scheduled to arrive the following summer, had just landed in Pohnpei. He wanted to survey the local conditions in advance of the entire medical team's arrival.

Ian was a phenomenon, a whirlwind, and all other work was suspended during his stay. Without speaking a word of their language, he coopted the attention of the four Pohnpeians who accompanied us: Sohn Alpet, his son-in-law, Pedro, and two health aides assigned by the hospital.

Due to the absence of roads into the heavily forested and mountainous regions outside Kolonia, walking would take several days, so we went by boat. We rented a typical Mokil whale boat, a type that has supplanted the single outrigger canoes of olden days. The whalers of the nineteenth century introduced this design from New England, and the sturdy, wide-bellied craft was easily duplicated by the skilled

27

boat builders of Micronesia. It carries eight to ten people comfortably, although one time I rode in one loaded with twenty-three people. Although the boats have oarlocks like the ones in *Moby Dick,* they are now powered by outboard motors. Two men navigated, one in the back with the outboard and one in front with a pole to guide the boat over shallow reefs and through the circuitous channels.

We boated into the Kolonia harbor, past the derelict, rusty landing craft left from the Japanese and American navies of World War II. As we followed the harbor markers into the lagoon, we had a spectacular view of Pohnpei from the water. Clouds hung over the central peaks which rose almost 3,000 feet above sea level. The tropical vegetation appeared even denser from this viewpoint than it did on land. The smell of the sea and the sounds of birds so celebrated in poems about the ocean thrilled our land senses. Every vista looked like scenes from the *National Geographic.*

Enthralled, I fantasized about the reactions of the first peoples who sighted and settled the island. As we continued through the ship channel cut through coral, I put on my hat, long-sleeved shirt, and sunscreen. The direct rays of the sun only a few degrees north of the Equator burn with a vengeance, even as they illuminate the exotic coral formations waving only a few feet below the surface of the turquoise water. We approached the fringing reef that protects the island and the lagoon from the ocean's relentless waves. The moods of the ocean beating against the encircling reef change with the weather or in response to events thousands of miles away.

Nearing the fringing reef, we sighted a ship that had been wrecked in a storm and impaled on the coral. Watching the gulls and terns that nested on the abandoned ship, I switched my fantasies to such favorite sea stories as *The Rime of the Ancient Mariner* and *Two Years before the Mast.* Fortunately, these romantic thoughts occupied me as the boat driver sped through the turbulence of the transitional zone between the lagoon and the open sea. The deeper hues and broad gentle swells of the ocean contrasted sharply with the lagoon. From this distance, no signs of human occupation were visible.

Normally I would panic over being in a tiny boat on a vast ocean. I have read too many lost-at-sea books. But I believed myself safely in the hands of descendants of the "Vikings of the sunrise." I loved Peter Buck's classic stories of the navigational genius of the Polynesians and their close relatives, the Micronesians. Theirs was the greatest seafaring achievement of all time. Those incredible sailors settled the far archipelagoes on the world's largest ocean while my European ancestors were still clinging to the shores of the Mediterranean in leaky boats.

Micronesian navigators sail by the stars and the subtle rhythm of currents as they break against the hull of a canoe. Through accidental and planned voyaging, their ancestors had colonized the habitable islands of the Pacific thousands of years before Magellan arrived. They sailed in families, using the strength of the young and the wisdom of the aged. Adapting to a seagoing life, they carried pigs, chickens, dogs, seeds and plantings for pioneering new lands. Voyaging on the ocean was their inheritance. I felt safe.

Ian, who was always serious about blood pressure, produced his portable cuff and took readings on all of us.

"Amazing," he said to me, "you have the lowest pressure and pulse on the boat. Aren't you nervous or excited at all?"

"Why should I be?" I explained my historic sense of security with the Vikings of the Pacific.

Then, through Jack's tactful translations of the conversation that followed, I began to intuit the purpose of the extra outboard motor, the cans of gasoline, the bottled water, and the food supplies on the floor of the boat.

"I never go outside the reef in a boat unless I have no other choice," revealed Sohn Alpet as he clutched his seat. "It is too dangerous. We have planned for emergencies, but you can never tell. I leave travel on the ocean to the outislanders who understand it."

The Pohnpeian fear of the open ocean was as great as mine! True, they had many legends about fleets of ocean-going canoes venturing to and from the islands. But those traditions were ancient and had since been lost. Modern Pohnpeians are landlubbers who use the lagoon only when necessary. Their pride is in farming skills and the fertility of land. They relied on people who came from the low-lying atolls to preserve and practice seafaring habits.

We had taken the boat into the ocean only because the lagoon passage to our destination would have been difficult to navigate in that period of low tides. Having circumvented that area by sailing beyond the reef and back into the lagoon, we shortened our trip. I dropped my fantasy life, vowed never to enter the open ocean again, and prayed to the God who protects naive anthropologists. Ian proudly reported that my pulse rate was climbing.

Once returned gratefully to terra firma, we spent several days hiking the mountain paths as Jack paid ceremonial visits, scouted the areas for our study, and introduced us to important people and old friends.

As we walked, our guides pointed out specific locations and explained various plants, although no one volunteered any information about their own gardens. The coconut palms looked as though they grew wild, but each one had an owner whose rights to fruit were respected by everyone. But the standards of Pohnpeian hospitality are high and the requests of strangers for a coconut to drink will be honored. The milk of the green coconut is delicious and more thirst-quenching than the soft drinks and sugar water preferred by the islanders themselves.

I saw green jungle, wild and uninhabited but for the occasional oasis of a homestead and surrounding clearing. Either because of the nature of the terrain or the force of tradition, Pohnpeians do not build what Westerners think of as communities. In Wene, there are no villages focused on a central public area. Homesteads, churches, the dispensary, docks, stores, and feast houses are scattered through the tropical forest and connected by seemingly random and winding paths.

The farms of which Pohnpeians are justifiably proud are simply not visible to the western eye. There are no plowed fields, no fenced gardens, no rows of crops.

On Pohnpei, every place has a name, an owner, and traditional stories about its special spirits or genealogical history. Pohnpeian eyes see gardens, boundaries, and a complex system of land tenure where I see only jungle. As Pohnpeians talked to me, I began to feel a growing pressure to understand and master these place names. The stories and legends I heard were less tales of the human passions I yearned for than lists of place names:

"This hero came from this place to that place and there in that place met another person who came from another place. Together they go off to yet another place [fully described]."

When legendary lovers succumb to passion, the place is specifically named. It was no accident that the first grammar lesson I learned was locatives, or words and word endings that told where we were going, where we had been, and whether the directions were up or down, over or under.

As we walked, Sohn Alpet commented, "Now we are leaving X and entering Y." But how could he tell, and how could he expect me to remember when landmarks were as absent as on the ocean? I probably never outgrew my frustration with having to learn so many place names. Eventually, I understood the importance that even a casual assortment of rocks along the shore had to Pohnpeians. Place names for Pohnpeians, as in many other societies, are markers or codes for historical events that explain why people are the way they are and why their relationships must be conducted in certain ways. An individual on Pohnpei is enmeshed in a web of kinship, titles, obligations, and social relationships that are literally grounded—tied to specific places with unique stories.

My tendency was to describe a place as down the path from that church, not far from this house, or over the next hill where the big rocks are. But all places, however bereft of identifying characteristics to me, have a name. As one lay minister explained, "What was the first job that God instructed Adam to do? Name everything!" When I protested that God had obviously meant for Adam to name animate objects, such as plants and animals, my instructor told me to reread the Genesis account and report back when I acquired greater wisdom.

For Pohnpeians, places have personalities and spiritual characteristics just as Westerners believe people do. The statuses, the title system, that Pohnpeians work so hard for are all tied to geographical locations. This viewpoint links seemingly unrelated information together. For example, a baby adopted from another clan can be made part of the adopter's clan by feeding it breadfruit from the adopter's land. So, people are in places, but places are also in people.

Place legends were easier to understand than the sheer number of place names. At one lovely high mountain pool below a waterfall, Sohn Alpet pointed out the eels swimming there and discussed the founding myth of the Lasialap, the Great Eel Clan, which he had inherited from his mother. The story cycle of the beginnings of the clan involves the extraordinary adventures of at least three generations of eels before the last generation magically gives birth to the female ancestors of the clan. Naturally, the adventuring eels traveled from place to place. I suspect that with all the places described, the story could take days to tell.

The story is long, complicated, and not to be told in its entirety. The conclusion is simple: because of the heroism and sacrifice of the eels in creating the clan deep in the past, members of the Lasialap clan are prohibited from eating the sacred creature. Breaking the taboo against eating the clan totem can bring down the punishment of the spirit world and the guilty may suffer. Jack believed that guilt over breaking such a taboo could induce a psychosomatic allergy or illness.

Our time in Wene was delightful, giving no hint of the problems we were to encounter later. We stayed in the house of one of the prominent citizens, also the health aide at the dispensary, whom I called Dr. Franko. The house had an elaborate water catchment system for cold showers. The house reminded me of the home of Hansel and Gretel, a lone dwelling in a primordial forest linked to others only by random rocky paths.

"Be careful," my host warned as I rose with the 5:30 dawn to take a walk before breakfast. "Ghosts may be on the path. Watch for a women who carries a basket of breadfruit on her left arm. You may look at her but do not speak. If you talk to her, she will have the power to take you away to the underworld where spirits live." I watched for her on my early-morning walks each visit to Wene. To my disappointment, she never appeared and I wondered if local spirits have reasons to avoid foreigners.

Belief in spirits is very much alive; in time, they felt like a sensible reality to me. Some places are so wondrous, some events are so difficult to explain, some happenings are so magical that how else are we to understand what we cannot see. On this island, there are spirits of the dead, clan spirits, spirits of certain places, spirits who just hang around, and spirits who are arranged in a systematic hierarchy just as people are.

Controlling the world of spirits requires magical incantations. Spells protect people, houses, crops, canoes, or dangerous ventures against natural or supernatural disasters. To make kava grow, to insure a good catch in the fishing nets, to make rain, and to stop rain require a blessing. Some of the practices are aimed at placating the spirit of deceased relatives. Others are love magic for successful amorous adventures. When relatives leave and return from a trip, they are anointed with oil. The ceremony may look like an ordinary welcome-home party, but actually it is a cleansing ritual to rid the travelers of foreign spirits.

Many of the spirits are localized, that is, they live only in their special places (which naturally have names). Others such as the mangrove demon, have a more extensive realm. Tiny trolls live in the high grasses of the rain forest. By living in wild, unsettled places outside the boundaries of daily living, the spirits help people define themselves as cultured, civilized, or ordinary.

The Pohnpeians say that in olden times people were unenlightened. They literally lived in darkness and in warfare. Now they claim (sometimes piously and sometimes sincerely) that they live in light, thanks to the coming of the Christian god and a spirit of cooperation. Although men seem glad to have given up the intermittent warfare that characterized their past, they have not given up the spirit world. The spiritual universes of Pohnpei exist beside the expansion of Christianity and have accommodated to, not receded with, the introduction of western religion. The God of Thunder still speaks with a mighty voice and brings good fortune to those who respect him, and mangrove demons still will cause illness and death if they are crossed.

I appreciated the wisdom of naming everything when I walked through the jungles at night. Place names seemed to tame the wildness and bring order to the green chaos. Nothing really dangerous exists on the island. Before human contact, no land mammals inhabited the place. Humans brought dogs and the ubiquitous rat. Since birds fly and fish swim, the variety of these species is not surprising. There are no snakes or deadly insects. A few types of fish are poisonous to eat; a few types of plants are said to be dangerous if prepared by a sorcerer.

However, some repulsive creatures have established a foothold. Giant African snails,introduced after World War I as a possible food source, proliferated in an ecology which had no natural predators to keep them in check. Those of us who admired French cuisine used to discuss ways to clean and cook them, but the Pohnpeians refused to eat them.

Attempts had been made to control the snails. The Japanese colonial administration organized school children to collect and destroy them. Then a predator was introduced in the hopes of checking their advance. This predator was a truly disgusting horned toad that soon discovered a more appetizing source of nourishment. Instead of eating the snails, the toads happily dine on the mounds of pig dung that litter the paths. I carried a flashlight at night, but stepping on them still was unavoidable. Although not fatal nor even painful, the feeling of spiky toads and squishy pig dung underfoot was terminally revolting.

On this first visit to Wene, I spoke little Pohnpeian. But I was learning to listen better each day. Sohn Alpet had a talent for phrasing simple sentences and stories. Despite Ian's protests about the transmission of dread diseases through kava drinking, I discovered that nightly kava poundings were a wonderful chance to practice speaking. In the relaxed atmosphere surrounding kava, we met people, talked about the project, and spoke the language with less strain.

I liked the stories that were spontaneously offered during these sessions, even though I received many warnings that everyone could not tell the stories correctly. I was told that any storyteller (other than the speaker) would embellish stories much as yams and other foods are decorated with leaves to make them look better. To me, however, a good story well told was even better for the flourishes of green leaves. My favorite at this stage were the stories told to children. These were appropriate to my simple language skills.

One evening I heard the tale of the origin of kava:

> People noticed that rats ate from the base of a certain plant. Then they could
> no longer run about but would stagger to sugar cane, eat some, and fall asleep.
> When people tried some of this plant, they became light-headed. The sugar
> cane that they also tried was delicious and sweet. Then the people of Heaven
> spied on the people of the Land and wanted to try some too, so two women
> stole a cutting and gave it to the Lords of the Eel, who planted it in the garden
> plot of Heaven. They harvested it. But as they prepared it, a piece of the root
> bounced out and fell onto the island, where it multiplied.

Once, kava was central to Pohnpeian religion, and the early Christian
missionaries tried to stamp out the practice. Today, Protestant elders usually do
not partake. But they expect others to drink; they affirm the spiritual value of
kava. They grow it, prepare it as a sacrament for others, but will not drink it.
Sohn Alpet continually touted its importance to me, although he had taken an oath
of abstinence himself. Catholics, on the other hand, had no history of abstinence.

With the first sip of kava, the lips and tongue grow numb. Speech is slowed,
but the head remains clear. Although heavy consumption may result in some
weakness or loss of control in the legs, the drink is not hallucinogenic, nor do
drinkers become drunk as with alcohol. The main effect is serenity and
peacefulness. People say, "You cannot drink kava and stay angry." This was a
pleasant change from the heavy drug cultures with their extravagant claims of insight
and the resultant hysterias, which were sweeping the United States at that time.

The kava ritual is hypnotic. One need not partake to appreciate its beauty. The
stones on which the roots of fresh kava are pounded are about three to four feet
in diameter and resound with a clear bell sound when struck. At formal feasts,
there are ancient rhythms that mark special parts of the ceremony. When kava
is made in homesteads on ordinary evenings, the sounds of the pounding carries
on the air, inviting any within hearing distance to participate.

The rhythm of pounding contrasts with the quiet talk. Since electricity did not
reach to the outer areas of Kolonia, the lighting was by kerosene lanterns or an
old-fashioned torch. The gestures of the men who pound, squeeze, and serve are
deliberate with the accumulated custom of centuries. Each movement at the stones
is slow and patterned. The rituals of serving the kava in coconut-shell cups follows
the etiquette and traditions of respect even in the simplest households. Women
may nurse children who then fall asleep in someone else's arms. Others bring
bits of food and stay to talk. Popcorn, fruit, sugar cane, candy, or little snacks
are eaten through the evening as the quietness of kava takes over.

When people are mad at each other, even when murder, adultery, or other serious
offenses have been committed, they will drink kava together at special feasts of
apology or propitiation. Because kava symbolizes public forgiveness and the
granting of pardon, they cannot remain angry or take revenge.

Because the drink induces heavy salivation, many drinkers will spit between the cracks in the floorboards or over the sides of the feast houses. After several slippery episodes I learned to stash my zories safely out of range of the acceptable habit of public spitting. My attempts to master the art of spitting were applauded, but I never learned to spit well.

One day we received an invitation to a household in the hills. The owner intended to open a pit that contained aged breadfruit. The rock-lined pit was about five feet deep and six feet in diameter. The breadfruit had been wrapped in leaves years ago and left in the pit to ferment. Like the casks of good bourbon, the age of the pit dated from the oldest portion, and keeping a pit going through several generations is a way to acquire status. Such preserved breadfruit may have served as famine food in the past. Jack lectured us on the history of this custom, and Sohn Alpet added comments on the proper manners for presenting it at feasts. Ian speculated on the public health implications and probable vitamin content. I ate some. It tastes like very ripe and exotic cheese. It certainly will never replace Hershey bars.

Ian, naturally charismatic, caused a stir wherever we went. He was well over six feet tall with a loud, booming voice and an irrepressible urge to offer medical advice. He often spoke Maori, the language of the Polynesians of New Zealand. Somehow he believed Maori to be the generic language of the Pacific. One night at kava drinking, he spotted a man with acromegaly (a pituitary gland condition that causes the extremities to grow rapidly and become deformed). Ian strode over the man, introduced himself loudly in Maori, and began to arm wrestle with him. Having determined the extent of the man's physical strength, Ian demonstrated a series of exercises for rehabilitation and pain management. The Pohnpeians, who understood no more Maori than the rest of us did, were deeply impressed. They have a long tradition of massage and exercise as healing techniques.

Ian's extroversion and Jack's legendary stature among the islanders helped put our research project on firm ground. With this trip to Wene, we laid the groundwork for the census, the sociological-psychological interviews, and the visit of the medical team, all of which would be spaced over the following year.

Roger and I needed to move. The relatively luxurious living in the Peace Corps house in Kolonia ended as Floyd left and Ian's visit was complete. Sohn Alpet arranged for us to move in with one of his daughters, Kioko, and her husband, Pedro. The house was a new, four-room cinder block, tin-roofed, slab construction that had been designed by bureaucrats in Washington as suitable for the tropics. I suspect that Micronesians favored these houses because they are cheap and appear modern. In reality, they are hotter, dirtier, and far less attractive than the raised, thatched and open stilt houses built of native woods.

This temporary living arrangement was a valuable opportunity to live in the Pohnpeian style and to work on the language. In the house, set randomly but closely to other houses of similar construction lived Kioko, Pedro, their ten children and a Peace Corps volunteer, Mike. The best way to describe their living arrangements is shifting, certainly flexible. Mike had been moved out of his room on our behalf, an acknowledgement of his acceptance by the family and probably a covert permission to court their beautiful daughter. Not all of the ten children were ever present at the same time. Some were staying with relatives in another district. Other family members came into Kolonia and stayed with Kioko and Pedro for periods of days, weeks, or months. Despite the nuclear-family appearance of the cinder block houses, the sleeping and eating arrangements were based on older, extended-family patterns. Cook houses, feast houses, outhouses, and other facilities were shared by several loosely related generations.

We washed from a rain barrel next to the house or from a community spigot across the muddy path. Latrines, or "little houses," were randomly situated for community use. A spring emerging from the rocky hillside provided bathing and laundry facilities. Women gathered there during the day, washed clothes, children, dishes, and themselves while preserving their modesty. Men usually went after dark, when there was greater privacy.

Our eating habits changed. We ate the family breakfast, which was a few bites of cold leftovers or ship biscuits (unsalted, unleavened hard crackers that originated as a staple on sailing ships). For snacks we ate bananas; the variety and taste were far beyond the common banana found in U.S. markets. I still miss the fat bananas, the short bananas, the sweet bananas, the tart bananas, the red, the orange, and the other varieties. Lunch was generally canned mackerel and rice. My only difficulty with the diet was a high-prestige drink made from about equal amounts of water, sugar, and food coloring. Finally, in desperation, I announced that I was getting the "sugar sickness" (diabetes) and must avoid sugar in that form.

Living in a Pohnpeian household enabled Roger and me to observe and discuss ordinary topics—mostly sex, children, and politics. We could have simple conversations with women working in one of the open cooking houses, which are their substitutes for porches.

"Who is watching your children while you are here?"

"Roger and I don't have any children yet."

"But you said that you were truly married in church. Why would you want to be married if you don't have any children? It is better to wait until you have children before you get married."

"It is the custom of my religion to get married first and then have children."

I was uncomfortable being quizzed about my personal life. I found it tricky to justify customs I followed but did not always accept, or customs I accepted but did not observe. I resorted to the same answer I often received, "Why do I do that? Because it is the tradition."

"Who is watching your pigs while you are here?"

"I don't have any pigs."

Childless, I was a target for sympathy and help, but pigless and landless, I was not a proper grown-up. They kept repeating the question until, finally, I changed the answer.

"Who is watching your pigs and land while you are here?"

"My mother [may she forgive me] is watching my pigs."

"Good, they are reproducing, and so you will have more of them when you return."

Of course, there was no reason for me to expect my companions of the cookhouses to be any more attuned to cultural relativism or any less ethnocentric than Floyd was. Being an inkblot for Floyd's misconceptions about anthropology was aggravating. Being an inkblot for some of the Pohnpeian women was data, information, and a way to do fieldwork. Nor could I maintain my notions of privacy when I wanted to ask them the same kinds of questions they asked me.

The conversations about having children grew more pointed. Concern for our childlessness increased, or began to be more overtly expressed.

"You should adopt a baby like other Americans who can't seem to have children. We will help you find one. What kind do you want? A boy? A girl? Newborn, toddler, teenager?"

This offer was quite serious and repeatedly made. Pohnpeians adopt each other's children or give children for adoption to foreigners with a generous spirit.

Women regularly offered me magical spells or chants believed to enhance fertility. They would remark that people in the olden times knew many spells for making babies or preventing them. They quickly added, "Of course, we ourselves are Christians now, and we don't use spells anymore. But we know some people who use them." Women without children wanted them passionately. Women with too many children frequently asked me about birth control. They all asked me about myself and about women in the States.

Everyone, male and female, agreed that I needed children. I could feel the pressure building as one said, "Babies are life's greatest blessing. We are going to have to help you. Don't you know that the ropes of marriage can part, but the ropes that bind children to parents are forever?" The last statement is a proverb similar to the saying that blood is thicker than water.

I was learning about family life and sexuality in gradual stages, just as I was to learn about politics or sorcery. I listened to lots of gossip, did a great many interviews, and exchanged personal information about myself before I appreciated that the sexual life of the island was more than a collection of exotic customs and techniques for making love.

Pohnpeians, like many other peoples in the world, regard sex with more fun and less seriousness than most Westerners do. The openness about sex in this island society reminds me of that reported by Margaret Mead in her famous book *Coming of Age in Samoa*. But talking about other peoples' sex lives may cause problems. The Samoans have not been happy with what Mead wrote about them. An occasional anthropologist thinks that she misinterpreted the whole culture. No matter what really happens or what they really do, Samoans, like others, wish to present a prim and proper front. Not all anthropologists on Samoa have collected the same information or reached the same conclusions about sexual life. The same is true for Pohnpei. Each anthropologist who has worked there has a different feel for the elephant. Some have far more lurid details than I to report; others choose to emphasize the Pohnpeians' public view of themselves as modest, discrete, and rule-abiding.

Pohnpeians are well aware that the Japanese, the Americans, and the church officials with whom they have lived for many years have different standards for sex and family life. In public, some insist that things have changed and that Pohnpeians are now abiding by the rules imposed by foreign influences. In private, however, they laugh, joke, and gossip incessantly about sex. In private, I think they are having ribald, exuberant, enthusiastic, playful sex lives.

In Pohnpei, as in small-scale societies anywhere, gossip and public shame keep people in line. The strongest control over sex or any other area of human life is not law or the formal control of governments. It is the fear of ridicule. It is gossip. The easiest way to learn what is expected and how to behave is to hear the gossip on who has done what, how, and with what consequences. This is why gossip is not a trivial activity, but one to which anthropologists pay close attention. In the United States, Jack never gossiped. But in the field, he often noted the power of gossip and recounted and analyzed stories we heard. He remarked that joking and gossip were both our main forms of entertainment and the stuff of ordinary life.

Learning about the clan system or the title system requires long extensive interviewing and cross-checking as anthropological research techniques. Learning about family life started the first time my childlessness was a topic for speculation. Learning about sex started the second night on the island when I heard the peepers.

The crunch of footsteps outside the window after midnight was hard to miss. A loose giggle in the dark signaled their presence on that second night and many more to come. I asked questions, but usually the information was volunteered. I learned that the boys posed no dangers. They were curious about foreigners. Although their nocturnal activities were not officially approved, they were certainly tolerated. In a curious way, the peepers were following traditions as they were supposed to do.

There is a word in Pohnpeian that translates as "walking about at night." In other societies in the Pacific, this practice is called night-crawling. A young man must brave a girl's sleeping household to rendezvous with her. Sometimes, they have made arrangements to meet in this romantic fashion. At other times, the boy has heard of the charms of a girl but has no close acquaintance with her. Favorite folktales and songs tell the story of a boy who hears of girl and overcomes great difficulties to be with her at night. Girls are reputedly thrilled to be the focus of such romance and bravery.

A boy who succeeds at night-crawling will be admired as splendid or beautiful. Naturally, young men brag to each other of their intimate conquests as they plan the next one and compare strategies. Occasionally, people will have more than one affair going at once. Although trysts are supposed to be a secret, calculated revelation and controlled gossip adds spice. Young women want to be courted, want romance and suitors, and yet want to control what is said of them. The dilemma is to be thought of as difficult rather than as easy, to attract the right man on the right night and to appear modest in public, yet exciting in private.

Judging from the gossip, the girl's relatives may assist the couple. If the family does not approve, it will place obstacles for the young couple. Once I had slept in many Pohnpeian households, I realized that sleeping arrangements are extraordinarily flexible. Everyone arranges his or her mat on the floor of the central room. Only honored guests or an aged relative are presumed to need privacy. Very few bedrooms are available and occupancy fluctuates. A girl or her family has latitude over the success and frequency of night-crawling participation. She might be sleeping in the middle of wakeful babies and watchful elders. Or she might be conveniently sleeping near an exit. She may also be trailing off to the little house at frequent intervals during the night. The lack of privacy makes innovation necessary.

Older men are expected to give up this practice. Night-crawling is reserved for the young. But older men tell fond stories about their experiences. They claim that in the past, boys bought spells or chants to keep the dogs from barking and revealing their presence to the sleeping household. Girls acquired love magic to lure boys and make them fall in love. One man told me about stringing dry, unhusked coconuts together to use as flotation devices so he could cross the lagoon to his lover at night. Another told me a terrifying experience of clumsiness. He inadvertently woke up his true love's uncle (her mother's brother) who demanded an explanation of why the boy was there. The youth replied, "Do you have a light for my cigarette?" The uncle gave him some matches and went back to sleep. This story is supposed to illustrate the need for an appropriate excuse to be prowling a strange house at night. To me, it pointed out the connivance of custom.

A German anthropologist named Hambruch visited Pohnpei in 1910 and reported that "sexual intercourse begins very early . . . before marriage there is complete freedom in sexual intercourse" (7ii:76). He implies that there are no rules, only sexual freedom. But rules exist, they are just different from the ones Hambruch knew in turn-of-the-century Germany. For example, I heard a lot of criticism about western standards of sexual behavior. Stories were repeated about irresponsible Peace Corps or military men fathering children with young girls. Particular kinds of clothing and styles of walking or sitting were interpreted as lewd and immodest. Even carrying a sleeping mat down the street would be worthy of comment. Comparative morality is a slippery issue.

Sexual freedom for romantic youth on Pohnpei has limits. Couples who have successfully arranged midnight trysts may not date as western youth can. They simply do not go out to eat or to the movies together. In keeping with strong Pohnpeian feelings about public displays of affection, they will not hold hands, hug, or go on a picnic with each other. If families approve in general, they do not mind the couple having sex in the yard at night. But when the couple adds board to bed, they are considered married.

Imagine the cultural conflicts this creates for Americans. People in the United States have casual standards for public interaction between males and females and more rigid rules for sexual activity. Boys and girls are expected to get to know each other through more or less supervised social activities. It is not expected that they will routinely begin their acquaintanceship with intercourse at her house. The Pohnpeians may tolerate a foreign male (like the Peace Corps worker) moving in with their daughter and behaving like a son-in-law. They are scandalized and fear for their daughter's reputation if she accompanies him to the movies or to a restaurant.

While parents may covertly accept the fact of nocturnal excursions, premarital intercourse, and an occasional baby, families place a high public value on marriage and want to prevent undesirable unions. Marriage is a gradual process growing slowly out of the adolescent years of freedom and experimentation. A man and a woman become a couple when they openly establish a joint residence, that is, they live together. If the families of both partners publicly recognize this fact, the relationship is a marriage.

The same is true for divorce. People say that if the couple has been living together (or apart) for six months or so, then the changed terms of the relationship make it legal. In the past, it was rare for young couples to set up housekeeping on their own and rarer still if the woman had no children. This is why many questioned me for setting up a household with a husband and no children. The couple usually lives on and off with several sets of relatives until the children are older.

Church leaders, both native and foreign, have wielded considerable pressure on officials to regularize and enforce marriage and divorce laws. But the terms for true marriage (married with the blessing of the church) and vain marriage (what is called common law marriage in the United States) show the reality in practice. The ancient customs, missionary teachings, Japanese law, and U.S.-imposed civil customs are confused and mutually contradictory. There is no question that marriage in a church or a civil ceremony or a certificate of divorce from a judge establishes a legal relationship. But many marriages and divorces are considered binding, although they are not always registered (births and deaths also may or may not be registered).

The decision of a couple to live together is determined by family pressures, romantic love, and religious loyalties. Families may oppose a prospective spouse on the grounds that he or she is of lower rank, is of higher rank, is lazy, is an outlander, drinks too much, or may be a drag on the family resources. Occasionally, the power of romantic love is so strong that a couple will brave the pressures of family and church to live openly with each other, raise children, and consider themselves married.

Sexual permissiveness, however, changes officially after marriage. The public party line about extramarital sex is that married couples are straight, modest, fruitful, and relatively faithful. By all accounts, however, adultery is as frequent as it is socially disruptive or attractive. In the past, adultery and sexual jealousy caused clan wars and local feuding. Jealousy and betrayal are the themes of many legends and gossip. Today, the question for unfaithful spouses is where to find privacy and how to keep gossip in check.

Again and again, as I listened to the gossip, I was aware of an attitude about sexuality that permeated Pohnpeian customs. When two people of the opposite sex are left alone, the inevitable will happen. The couple will shrug, "what can we do, how can we help themselves?" A glimpse of an inner knee, a liquid look, and making love must begin. This may also be a tacit testimony to the vulnerability of women alone and a male rationale for forced sex. The solution is not increased internal control but the avoidance of occasions for incest or adultery.

When I collected data about incest, many of the stories concerned unusual combinations of forbidden relatives who find themselves alone together (on a deserted path, up a coconut tree, or even in a sinking canoe). The drive that will bring two people together in carnal knowledge is stronger than the fear of gossip or of breaking a taboo. Islanders watch each other, wise in the ways of physical attraction. If you do not wish to be gossiped about, stay near others. When a male and a female are seen together, the suspicion of intimacy will arise. I was chided several times for being seen alone with one of the interviewers. The interviewers made nervous jokes if we found ourselves alone together.

Pohnpeians are great strategic thinkers, in sex as in politics. The bottom line is that no matter what a man and a woman do or avoid doing, someone will find reason to suspect an affair. When a man and a woman want to be alone together, they will hide the fact. The immediate assumption is that if two people are successfully avoiding each other, they probably have something planned! Then again, they may *not* be avoiding each other to throw off suspicion in case someone should notice them avoiding each other.

The corollary to the principle of sexual opportunism is the principle of sexual necessity. Micronesians in general believe that everyone must have sex regularly. They also believe that no matter what anybody says, human beings cannot remain faithful or go without sex for extended periods of time. The third principle is mutuality. Women and men equally find pleasure in sex and in each other.

Gossip, it should be obvious, is one of the best sources of information in such a society. The language has a wonderful word which translates as "it is said," or "they claim." Placed at the front of the sentence — "It is claimed that men get bent penises from that activity," — the phrase absolves the speaker of responsibility. I have missed that word.

The statistics that Westerners consider research do not exist in a place like Pohnpei. Many or most marriages, divorces, births, or other forms of information about a population have never been registered. Attitudes and practices about sex, for example, cannot be collected by getting random subjects to fill out questionnaires. Only if an anthropologist lives in the community, speaks the language, hangs out with different groups, attends rituals, asks questions, answers questions, and listens, will she learn. Through time, the patterns that are so interwoven into the culture will be clearer. Only then is it possible to know that, for Pohnpeians, virginity does not carry the same meaning or economic value that it does in patrilineal societies. Only then is it possible to understand that members of the same clan help each other erect houses, give feasts, and discipline wayward clan mates.

Roger was like sticky fly paper for gossip about sex. Perhaps his innocent air or his study on healing attracted so many disclosures. On the other hand, it may have been his avid curiosity. His field notes are full of material, sometimes recorded as hearsay, but frequently as direct confessions or personal revelations. Both of us attracted questions about ourselves and American sex life in general.

Some of the Peace Corp volunteers used Roger as an older brother or confidante about their personal relationships. Everyone gossiped about the volunteers, particularly about young men who were entranced by the seeming flexibility of sexual customs. One volunteer confessed his night-crawling activities with chagrin. He made arrangements through a go-between to visit his lady love late at night. But he made some classic errors. First, he carried a flashlight, thus advertising his presence. Second, he had not scouted in advance the paths leading to her house. A local prankster, himself on the prowl, hid in the foliage and jumped out suddenly with machete in hand. Terrified, the volunteer youth ran wildly, fell, and tore his trousers and one knee. He limped for several weeks as the prankster told the story with glee.

Another Pohnpeian man, sophisticated and educated, had been squiring a Peace Corps woman in the western style to movies, restaurants, and other public occasions. This meant only one thing: they were married. Then, as the woman finished her tour of duty and departed, she kissed him good-bye at the airport. That did it. By the time we heard the tragic tale, the embellishments and green leaves were fully in place. Here were star-crossed lovers who could never be reunited. She had joined a convent, died of a broken heart or an incurable disease, committed suicide, or succumbed to parental disapproval. Occasionally, I heard that she was locked in a tower. All of the young man's subsequent actions (including an ordinary marriage, a job, and cute kids) were explained by the tragic loss of his American wife.

Another U.S. volunteer had been living with a Pohnpeian man with the approval of his family. Thus, they were married without a church ceremony. Then she was seen in Kolonia in the company of other men, colleagues in the Peace Corps and Micronesians with whom she worked. The family was incensed and broke up the relationship. The young man was said to have accepted his family's evaluation of her actions. He wrote several bitter love songs about his feelings for her betrayal. Each time one of the songs aired on the radio, I heard another version of the story. It is easy to understand how legends of lost love are created.

Living in households with small children gave me natural chances to observe attitudes toward sexuality. I saw daily practices that contribute to the gentle but pervasive sexuality that I think marks Pohnpeian life. Sexual life is not hidden from children. Sleeping arrangements lack privacy. As long as the taboos about discussing sex in front of certain relatives are followed, adult conversations in the inevitable presence of children are frank. Children are teased about sex and are witness to more ordinary sex play than their peers in the United States are. Babies and toddlers do not wear clothes. Naked children play in groups. Curious children lurk silently near laughing adults and hear everything. I think of these daily interactions as the Pohnpeian version of sex education in which anatomy, physiology, and function are less important than an easy knowledge, spirited feelings, and a respect for family life.

Another story impressed me about the value systems of sexuality. A young girl named Maria began exhibiting the habits of a boy as she grew into her teens. She began to go walking about at night looking for girls. The activity itself was acceptable, but a girl doing it caused consternation. Family and neighbors held a meeting to discuss the problem. Then they held a feast where they publicly declared her a boy. Her hair was cut and she was presented with male clothing. Henceforth, they announced, Maria would be Mario. I heard that Mario became a responsible citizen with a wife and children.

The important fact about the story is not the cause of Maria's problems. The biological or psychological roots of his/her identity can only be surmised. Sometimes in human societies children are missexed (assigned to the wrong gender category). What fascinates me is the ease with which this mistake was repaired. Here was a sensible social solution to a sexual dilemma.

A few things, in the Pohnpeian view, are wrong. One of the principal sexual offenses is called "spying at the water." Young boys hide and spy on women as they bathe in pools or streams. The occasions on which boys spy on females are limited only by their imagination. I heard the noise of peepers dozens of times and caught groups and individuals in the act of spying. Other women tell similar stories. When I went to a remote pool to bathe, I could be certain boys were hidden in nearby groves of trees. This behavior is shameful because it is said to involve solitary sexual activity and to indicate an inadequacy in the males' ability to attract women.

It is also considered shameful for a man to take a woman by force. Something is seriously wrong with a man who has to do that. However, in every society, there are a few rotten eggs whose behavior cannot be condoned. The difference is that on a small island most people know who the bad characters are and avoid them. In a culture in which men gain sexual favors through good manners and do not reward their peers for aggression against women, rape is rarer than in the United States. I have heard that the incidence of rape as well as successful prosecutions have increased since I lived there. I was never warned off certain people, activities, or places, although I did get such warnings in other places I have lived.

The issue becomes murky in the area of crossed signals or how consent is conveyed. Some Pohnpeian men, just like some U.S. men, maintain that women say no but mean yes. Being alone, either purposively or accidentally, may imply consent. It is, however, perfectly permissible, even necessary, for Pohnpeian women to be explicit in rejection: "You stink," for example. Disparaging references to the man's private parts are also recommended. Less definite rejections can be interpreted as acceptance.

There is a Pohnpeian word meaning "to pick too young," which refers to the appropriate age for intercourse to begin. The ages customarily mentioned are lower than most Westerners find comfortable. The lower limit of sexual activity for girls was variously placed at eleven to fourteen years of age, certainly by fifteen to nineteen for conservative folk. It is generally assumed that intercourse is appropriate if a girl has started to menstruate and is not exposed to any situation that would harm her, emotionally or physically. Boys usually begin their sexual lives later than girls as their bodies are believed to mature more slowly.

The next question foreigners usually ask is, "But what if she gets pregnant?" The answer is incredibly simple. In Pohnpei, children are highly valued. Illegitimacy is not even a word. Children automatically belong to their mother's clan. So they have a social affiliation that only marriage gives in U.S. society. Children will have many males and females in their extended family to love and care for them. The man who weds their mother is considered their father. In fact, pregnancy is the reason a couple will regularize their union and settle down. A woman may select a mate during or even after her first pregnancy. The practice of adoption serves to reduce the pressures of unwanted pregnancy. Obviously, a century and a half of exuberant contact between the islanders with their easy sexual mores and foreigners resulted in babies. All of them are absorbed easily into their clans and families.

The outstanding characteristic of the value system of family life on Pohnpei is the warm practicality. It sounds so obvious and trite to say that children should be highly valued or that sexual activities should be frequent, discrete, mutually satisfactory to both partners, and harmful to no one, but those values are at the center of Pohnpeian culture.

Sometimes Westerners naively refer to places such as Micronesia as "primitive" or simple. Sometimes the Pohnpeians blame their current problems on U.S. colonialism. Most of the time Westerners and Pohnpeians alike tell anthropologists that the past was a golden time of rich rituals and reverence for custom, when life's meanings were clear and all children respected their elders. None of these folk beliefs are true.

Pohnpeian society before western contact was anything but simple. It was a politically sophisticated, hierarchically organized society with overseas trade links with the Truk Islands to the west and the atolls to the east. Nan Madol is an eloquent testimony to ancient Pohnpeian feats of engineering and organizational skills. Following foreign contacts in the early nineteenth century, the islanders managed to incorporate into all this complexity new iron technologies, western goods such as guns and alcohol, monetary trade, and most profoundly, the messages and organization of Christianity.

In the early 1800s, warfare made travel across the island dangerous. Clan ties were more important than they are now because they offered protection in places outside one's home community. The Pohnpeians say that the centuries before the coming of the missionaries in 1852 and the pacification of hostilities between the municipalities was a time of darkness in contrast to the current age of enlightenment. Their stories of intermittent warfare and political treacheries make this claim more than Christian propaganda.

The United States has not been the only colonist on the island. The rule of the Spanish from 1886 to 1899 produced little change, as they seemed frightened of natives and stayed in their fort. The ruins still grace Kolonia. The German administration, which lasted until the outbreak of World War I, brought a reduction in the powers of the Paramount Chiefs through the prohibition of warfare and changes in the ways people owned and inherited land. The Japanese influence over their colonial possessions in Micronesia lasted until their defeat at the end of World War II and will be deeply felt until the last generation of Pohnpeians who knew them are dead.

U.S. influence, however, does not date only from 1945 and the trusteeship. Americans were in Micronesia in the 1830s when whaling ships and trading ships stopped in Pohnpei. Pohnpeians have had extensive contact with the West for a century and a half. That change has been continual no one disputes. The relative contribution of these changes—the pleasures, the pains, the causes and the effects on Pohnpeian life—will continue to be studied, interpreted, and debated by anthropologists, historians, and administrators.

Despite one hundred and fifty years of contact with foreigners, the Pohnpeians have not given up their traditional politics, language or family organization. Adjusting to the succession of colonial governments, they have absorbed large numbers of other Micronesians into their cultural vision. Changes, though, were unavoidable. Foreigners brought the gospel; they also brought new and deadly diseases. A smallpox epidemic in 1854 wiped out at least half of the population. Venereal diseases, imported by the sailors and traders who thought themselves in a sexual paradise, are still endemic. Tuberculosis, leprosy, respiratory infections, and such childhood diseases as measles, wreak havoc on the health of islanders who have no natural immunity to the pathogens.

Even the material goods that islanders coveted from contact with whalers and traders altered traditional culture. Tobacco, firearms, knives, and alcohol brought germs of destruction as dangerous as diseases. Today, many observers say that some of the dangers of the twentieth century and the colonial administration originate in the subtle effects of such imports as transistor radios, canned foods, guns, and alcohol.

Outward appearances can be deceiving. Pohnpeians are comfortable with and sophisticated about western technology. They move easily back and forth between modern things and ideas and older traditions, often weaving complex new patterns. That does not mean, however, that people who wear the same clothes or drink the same beer as Westerners do think the same way.

Pohnpeians often speak of themselves in the past as pagans living unenlightened in a Dark Age. At the same time, they see themselves as deeply rooted in the land and in customs that change even as they remain the same. They lament the rootlessness of Americans and what they see as the shallowness of American customs and history. They had no choice about the arrival of foreigners, but they do choose how to adjust and to adapt. One of the great oral historians of Pohnpei, Luelen Bernart, explained the early history of contact with Westerners.

> Now the foreigners wandered about Ponape to no purpose and had no fixed place. They also had no work, for they did not accept the practice of Ponapean customs which were unenlightened. This is why the Ponapeans came to think that this was the way all foreigners were, and used to use them as bad examples. They would say, "How like you are to a foreigner who is stupid and lazy, begging and treacherous," . . . . The inhabitants of Ponape did not like foreign ways, clever ways or right ways, for it was their own ways that they liked. This is why they were slow in becoming accustomed to the foreign rule and the rule of Christianity (p. 106-107).

A letter from the field:

> Dear Len and all University of North Carolina supporters of high blood pressure,
>
> The questionnaire development is going very well and we have started preparations for the census. A separate budget sheet is attached. Thanks for all your efficiency in calling Washington to find out how we can buy pigs out of our budget. Glad you know how to switch budget categories so the project can make appropriate contributions.
>
> I have had to change my manner of dressing. Thank goodness for the Sears catalogue. Those minidresses and short skirts you all are wearing in the States cause quite a stir here. It seems that breasts are only normal female equipment for feeding babies. Clothing for many women consists of a large towel or three-yard length of brightly colored cloth. This is worn around the waist inside the house or in the yard, but is pulled up to cover your breasts for walking in the road. More formal dress is a one-piece dress with gathered waist (no doubt missionary inspired). The back zipper is rarely used except for church and community gatherings. If you have on a bra, you don't need a blouse. If you wear a blouse, then you don't need a bra. In fact, bras are considered proper public dress for women. Those black Maidenforms with the heavily stitched pointed cups are particularly valued.
>
> When foreigners are not around, it is sufficient to cover oneself only from the waist down. Jack says I should do what I feel comfortable with. I hope he means me to follow my Oklahoma-born inclinations and stay dressed. The

Pohnpeians ask, "Why do you wear a blouse and a bra at the same time?" I hope they are just teasing me.

Breasts are not particularly erogenous. But legs are. Particularly that sexy place on the inside of the knees. No more miniskirts for me. Fitting in and observing local custom means that I have unfashionably lengthened my skirts to below the knee. I have a proper slip that has a two-inch layer of hand crocheted embroidery on the bottom. Bright blue, red, and yellow flowers. The slip is designed to show below my dress. Later I will tell you other uses for this slip which has turned out to be most practical.

The American men watch women with nothing on above the waist. The Pohnpeian men comment on American women with short skirts. They eye our knees. I am now dressed to please the standards of two cultures.

You would love it here. Both women and men say that I am too skinny — downright scrawny for a proper woman. They expect women to eat a lot, gain weight, keep weight on after each pregnancy, and stay on the large side of pleasantly plump. They say, "Women eat to bear children." Even the posture of women is accentuated to make them look substantial. Men are compared to brown doves, a bird which eats a bite of fruit, leaves it and goes to another, always to nibble sparingly. Warriors in the olden days went to battle with an empty stomach. To die with food in one's stomach would have been humiliating. So men are noticeably thinner. Men who eat too much are subject to ridicule and women who are rotund, Rubenesque, roly-poly are objects of sexual interest.

You may think this discussion is about sex (again). Not so. File this information away. We will need it for the medical questionnaires and interpretations about blood pressures, weight, eating habits, and values.

I hear the plane coming in to land. If I hop on the motor scooter and hurry down to the airport, I can get this letter off the island.

Kasehlehlia.

- 3 -

Water Running
under Boulders

Concerning the various kinds of evil magic which the people of Pohnpei perform among themselves when they are feeling ill towards each other, these have their origin in the supernatural power of people:

Destruction: bury magical objects under the corner of an enemy's house
Making blood flow: people will die
Swimming fire: send flames from burning coconut leaves to one's enemy
Clouding the water: magical infusion and spells in the streams where a victim bathes — may cause blindness.

—from Luelen Bernart

A home at last. What a relief it was to move into Jack's spacious, shady, private house. After several months of shifting about, Roger and I needed an office, a retreat, and a real home, even a fixer-upper. With the departure of Jack, Ian, and Floyd, we were alone to run the research project until the arrival of the medical team the following summer. I began to see less a decrepit hut and more of a nest to build.

The wooden, tin-roofed house, exclusive of its three ad hoc additions, was one room about eighteen feet by eighteen feet with partitions to create visual privacy. We slept on mats on the floor and used a low Japanese table for working and eating. I adjusted to living on the floor, although I never learned to cook sitting down, as Pohnpeian women do with such skill. We painted, strung some fabric across the screens, and built a few bookshelves.

The house felt like a castle to us. I had not realized the advantages of living on a homestead. Sohn Alpet brought some of his relatives who explained each

49

of the plants in the yard, which also was an invaluable language lesson. We had a papaya tree, a breadfruit tree, a coconut tree, and a lemon-lime tree. Taro, the delicious Pacific root crop, grew in the yard, too. There were flowers, bushes, and shrubs growing in profusion, including a plant that yielded incredibly redhot peppers. The chickens that ate them tasted spicier than other chickens. According to custom, each food-bearing tree had a private owner, that is, the person or his or her descendants who originally planted the tree. We rented the homestead but had to negotiate for rights of use from the tree owners, who also gathered produce from time to time.

The electricity, one light socket and a plug, was illegally wired from the jail on the hill above the house. When it worked, we operated a fan. The Japanese had built a telephone system, but along with their other public works, the system had fallen into disrepair. We used gossip, little kids, and the motor bike as our primary means of communication.

The shower was a tin room paved with pieces of coral rock. It was about five feet square with a raised rock in the center for pounding clothes. The water for the shower and a small tin sink in the kitchen lean-to apparently came from the Kolonia system, which everybody tapped into at will with pipes running hither and yon. We were never billed for this water. The city of Kolonia had no drainage system for this part of town, so water from bathing and washing ran under the house and out into the yard.

The water was cold. For hot water, we heated some in a sauce pan on the two-burner butane stove in the kitchen. This gas stove was a major improvement over cooking with the kerosene camp stoves I had been using: less smell, less mess, and more ease of regulation. I learned to use a square biscuit tin placed on one of the burners as an oven. The cakes I continued to bake tasted awful, but homesick Americans appreciated them. I rarely bothered to heat water to wash dishes or to bathe. To rinse dishes, I put them in the middle of the kitchen floor and threw water on them. The water ran through holes in the floor, thereby cleaning dishes and floor.

Ian had sent a kerosene refrigerator and freezer manufactured in Norway. Trust the Norwegians to invent something so practical, although the directions for installation and maintenance were difficult to read. The medical team needed refrigeration for blood and urine samples, as well as their laboratory materials. We used it pending their arrival, although we had to sacrifice valuable floor space to accommodate the bulky piece. One of us had to be constantly vigilant and take care of the wicks and fuel levels, and the appliance required babysitting when we were away. On top of that, Kerosene stinks. Why bother? Because it made cooking in the tropics easier, and above all, the thing made *ice*. Beautiful, cold, crystal *ice*. Like most Americans, we took ice for granted, denied our addiction, and had trouble adjusting to ice deprivation. Our hut became a popular hangout when we started serving ice water to guests.

But the pièce de résistance, a marvel of U.S. ingenuity, was the toilet. Only a few privileged households and offices in town had regular flush toilets. The islanders built outhouses. But the public health saying, "flies, fingers, food, feces," describes the four-cornered cause and effect for the spread of disease in areas of the world that do not have adequate sanitation or running water. The outhouses with their constant flies that respected no boundaries were a source of dysentery and other illnesses that had plagued these islands since contact. No sewer treatment system had been built and the discharge of raw sewer into the harbor undoubtedly contributed to the growing incidence of hepatitis, parasites, and other waterborne diseases.

In recognition of the public health problems, the United States government had published a pamphlet on how to build an innovative toilet called the water seal. Jack, devoted to practical solutions, ordered the booklet from Washington and convinced Roger and me to built one. We hired workers to dig a hole about the size of a fifty-gallon drum. The hole was filled with rocks graded in size from large at the top to small at the bottom. This was a filtration system that needed no chemicals or outlets. The porous rocky ground of the island provided excellent drainage and filtering. The hole was capped with a tin lid and a layer of dirt and connected by a pipe to the third lean-to, which housed the toilet.

The toilet was only a square of concrete on the floor with an almond-shaped hole in the middle. A U-pipe connected the hole to the filtration system. Fresh water stayed in the base of the U-pipe, preventing smells from backing up from the rocky filter (hence, a water seal.) It flushed with water from a fifty-gallon drum that caught rainwater from the roof. The catchment system was connected to the toilet with a twenty-cent length of rubber hose that acted as a syphon.

To use the toilet, one squatted down and then sucked on the end of the hose to bring water from the rain barrel. No flies, no smell, no plumbing bills, no walks in the rain to the outhouse, and no public health hazards.

I was the only one who admired it. The Pohnpeians always discretely excused themselves and went across the road to an outhouse. Americans whose government had promoted this idea were shocked and insecure with the water seal toilet. They urged us to build a wooden seat, but I declined. I felt patriotic pushing the merits of the water seal toilet, but I wondered if the bureaucrats in Washington understand the cultural barriers to its adoption.

After one of the prisoners from the jail behind the house broke into the house to steal, Sohn Alpet brought us a puppy. I named him Pwutak (male youth). He had black and white spots, ate leftovers, and earned his keep by guarding the house. A wild cat named Yapper lived in the rafters of the house and dealt harshly with rodents. With time and regular food, she finally would come down from her perch, uttering her strange cry. At night she quietly deposited dead rats and mice in the same spot in the middle of the floor. A starved, flea-ridden orange cat called Oang-Oang (Yellow) wandered in and stayed to hunt the tiny mice Yapper missed. Unfortunately, both cats caught geckos, harmless little lizards with tiny suction cups on their feet that walk on the ceiling and walls harmlessly eating mosquitos. The mosquito population increased, and we had to burn green mosquito coils at night. Such are the perils of an ecologically balanced household.

The large yard held the framework of a classic Pohnpeian feast house with platforms on three sides and a kava stone in the middle. But the thatched roof had rotted. Although I loved the sound of rain on its tin roof, the house was uncomfortable on sunny days. So we negotiated with the landlord for a new thatch. We were learning how to conduct business in the local style. Roger's field notes reveal a righteous indignation, so we probably offended a number of people and paid too much. But it was worth the money just to watch a master craftsman weave and apply the ivory-palm thatch and later to sit under its cool rustle. Much of Pohnpeian life is conducted in feast houses. We began to use it as they did, as office, guest room, dining room, study, and den.

Our schedule was simple. The sounds of clothes pounded with wooden paddles woke us up. The Micronesians, with habits formed by centuries of early bedtimes and no electricity, rise with the sun. By 8 a.m. our interviewers were eager to work. We did at least three hours of language study a day in addition to correspondence, meetings and shopping.

Soon after the move into new quarters, a gardener adopted us. Although mystified by the demands of horticulture in the tropics, I was insecure about creating an image of colonialism by hiring people to wait on me. Ioannes just appeared one day and started cutting and weeding. Put on the payroll, he proved an invaluable addition to our growing staff. A shy and loving man, he had been born and raised in the Mortlocks, atolls in the Truk district. There he had learned traditional forms of diagnosis, treatment, and curing of disease. His specialty, indeed his genius, was in ancient forms of massage as a curing and healing technique.

Ioannes decided to teach Roger what he knew about healing, divination, and curing, which fit into the traditional medicine study. Ioannes showed me how to get rid of muscle spasms, cramps, indigestion and other ordinary ailments. He had some potions and oils for insect bites and an instant cure for centipede bite. Beyond the immediately practical, which I found comforting, he knew the theories of the relationship between the body and mind on which all native treatments of disease are based.

Sohn Alpet, with his baseball cap and black briefcase, tried to look casual when he dropped by our homestead on the weekends. But his visits always had a special agenda. One evening he complimented us on our diligence in studying Pohnpeian. "However," he commented, "you speak like children. You know the words and sentences, but you do not use the respect language for high people. I shall have to teach you."

The truth is that he did not trust Akina, the linguistic informant we had been using. Akina was, for various complex reasons, beyond the point of paying homage to men or to customs from which she derived no benefit. Although she had lived on Pohnpei, married, worked, and raised her many kids there, she had not been born on the island and was not connected to the local version of the old-boys' network. As he viewed the situation, the sharp tongue and irrepressible intelligence that made her so suitable for language study, meant that we were not being schooled in the codes of deference valued by Pohnpeians.

Basically, there are three levels of language usage: common, then respectful, and honorific. The latter two levels together are called "high language." Because the Pohnpeians value sophisticated oratory and skilled speech, there are subtle gradations between these levels. I tried unsuccessfully to convince Sohn Alpet that as a mere woman I had no occasion to talk to high-ranking people. Let Roger sweat it out. Alternatively, I would keep Sohn Alpet at my side to translate properly. But Sohn Alpet was having no part of my playing liberated professional one moment and dutiful, retiring wife the next.

The initial problem is a special vocabulary. Such ordinary actions as eat, speak, love, hate, die, come, go, sleep, think, weep, wash, and whisper have substitute words in either the respect form or the honorific form or both. Most body parts (literally from head to toe) and nouns for common places (cookhouse, canoe, eating place, bathing place, pillows and many others) have different words, depending on the level of honor intended.

In addition, other words have no meaning except to show status. I call these words of humiliation and exaltation. Their purpose is to symbolically elevate other people and their possessions while belittling yourself and your possessions. A loose translation (which is the only kind possible) may convey the flavor. "Would your honored self deign to give this unworthy person something to drink [special word for drink]?"

Just learning more vocabulary is not that difficult. The challenge is to know *when* and *to whom* to speak. The purpose of these special ways of talking is to show respect, so every social interaction must be judged in terms of the relative status of those speaking. The form of speech depends on how you view your own social rank in relation to others (including those who are only the topic of conversation).

Talking to or about another person is difficult. Knowing the language is not enough. A thorough knowledge of the entire title system and related customs of respect is essential. In fact, advancement into the high ranks of the society requires mastery of these linguistic forms. Not even older Pohnpeian men use these forms with equal facility.

The levels of saying thank you are only the beginning. Informally, to children or pets, you can say *menlau* or "hey, thanks." For older people and those with higher rank, depending on how you assess that, you say *kalahngan en kowmi*. For younger people and peers, just *kalahngan* or the phrase *mehn sahmwa* is appropriate. Other phrases of gratitude must be used for the Paramount Chiefs, for God, and for the spirits.

It is not just a matter of convenient phrases such as "your exalted pig" or "my humble pig." This society has extraordinary political complexity with very few

visible markers to indicate who the high people are. They do not wear crowns
or jewels or drive fancier cars. The privileges of rank for them are in the seating
arrangements and the distribution of food at feasts and, above all, in clever and
sumptuous displays of language. They know each other's genealogies, recent title
promotions, and other rationales for ranking. I had to learn.

It is impossible to utter a worthwhile sentence without taking a stand on the
amount of respect due to those being addressed. Besides title and rank, the questions
of relative age and kinship are also important. Sohn Alpet insisted that we address
him by his title, Nahnihd Lapalap, and use respect language to him and others
he designated. He did not care about teaching us nouns, verbs, or new sentence
structures; he cared about the language of respect. This was very difficult for me.
Even when I knew appropriate forms and the status of the person I was addressing,
my prairie-born soul rebelled.

The instruction in high language was my tradeoff with Sohn Alpet. I had spent
hours and days under the thatch roof of our feast house training him and his assistant
Roswel in the strange mysteries of western social science. We discussed how and
why to do a household census, how and why we needed a sample, and why blood
pressure was related to how people act and feel. We also planned the next phase
of the research project, which meant completing the census and beginning the
questionnaires in the municipalities of Kitti, U, and Madolenihmw. Sohn Alpet
and I were investing heavily in each other: he with the protocols of respect, and
me with the demands of interdisciplinary research.

First on our agenda was a return trip to Wene on the other side of the island.
Working out the living arrangements and the payments for room and board there
had been tricky. Sohn Alpet had a high title from Madolenihmw. If he stayed with
anyone who had a lower title, the man would be obliged to give him an expensive
feast. If he stayed as a guest of someone with a higher title, we would have to
pay for a feast. On the previous visit, we had arranged (or so we thought) to pay
room and board based on the rate the Peace Corps paid, which was less than hotels
in Kolonia charged. We had been assigned a fairly high status as foreigners, but
I suspect that was a canny assessment of the project's budget.

Although we planned to leave on Monday, rain, boat troubles and missed
appointments postponed our departure. It was late Tuesday afternoon when we
arrived at our host's farmstead, sunburned, drenched, and hungry. Several hundred
people filled the house, feast house, and yard. A funeral for a high-ranking section
chief (our host's father's brother) had reached a crescendo. The Paramount Chief
of Kitti was already seated and other high-ranking dignitaries from Madolenihmw
were expected momentarily.

The *kamadipw,* feast, was a triple celebration: the commemoration feast for the
deceased man, the title payment feast for his successor, and a housewarming
("cleansing of worms") for the new feast house fortunately completed just days
before. Although this was a splendid ethnographic opportunity, the project was
swamped in ceremonies and we were homeless. A funeral feast for a newborn

baby had been held that Sunday night, so few people in Wene had slept much for the previous three nights.

Although I had attended kava poundings and family feasts, this was the first truly traditional feast of such magnitude that I witnessed. The demands of protocol, hard physical labor, and the stress of obligations were evident in the Pohnpeians' composure. Sohn Alpet had been assigned a place close to the front, where high-titled Pohnpeians were seated. He whispered hurried instructions. "Show respect to the high people and elders. Always, no matter how uncomfortable you are, sit crosslegged on the platform and never, never, dangle your legs off. Don't get up and leave because you don't know the right speeches to ask to be excused."

All feasts in Pohnpei follow an ancient pattern. Kava plants are presented, prepared, and served in accordance with prescribed rituals. At the open end of the feast house, an earth oven is built and foods are steamed. The earth oven contains breadfruit, yams, and pigs. There are always speeches announced by a master of ceremonies whose job of protocol management looks taxing. I could barely see the Paramount Chief of Kitti who sat with his back to the wall at the head of the feast house with wife, retainers and others of high rank arrayed below him.

A word about the custom of eating dogs: Dogs were a major source of protein, along with fish, for Pohnpeians and other Pacific islanders before contact with Westerners. Now they are only used ritually, that is, in connection with feasts. Specialists prepare them, wrapping them in a certain type of leaf binding and cutting the meat in prescribed ways. Only certain men know these skills. Serving dog marks honorific, even liturgical occasions. Nowadays, pork is more frequently used for family gatherings and in daily diets. In fact, pigs have an economic importance dogs do not have. But dog remains a ceremonial option. Pohnpeians know that Westerners do not eat dogmeat and courteously offered us the choice to partake or not.

In the wake of the funerals, the arrangements for housing and meals we had negotiated were void. Hurried agreements took advantage of our inexperience and need. We found housing in a homestead about an hour's walk into the hills. A Peace Corps couple lived in the same homestead, and their plight was probably worse than ours. Their host overcharged them mercilessly while insisting that such payments were only observances of the local customs. They were slowly going broke and were grateful to compare notes with foreigners whose gullibility was greater than theirs. The only other foreigners in Wene were friends of ours, an anthropologist from Ohio State University, his wife and their two small children. Due to the complexity of their negotiations about living arrangements, they were all sharing one small room in Dr. Franko's house, where we had stayed before. During this time, we missed a few meals and caught others where we could.

The morning after the triple feast, which had lasted very late, we met with Dr. Franko, the health aide at the dispensary, to plan the census and the logistics of the month's work. Sohn Alpet and Roswel departed with forms in hand. Two hours later, Roswel returned. An announcement on the radio called for all the relatives of his wife's sister to gather for her funeral. We loaned him travel money and he left.

Six days later, he had still not returned. Sohn Alpet was feeling ill and Roger had the flu. I was irritable and vexed at Roswel. But when Roswel finally showed up, Sohn Alpet pleaded that the poor kid had family troubles, a pretty young wife with a new baby, and a sick father. Roswel had to walk back to Wene from Kolonia, a hard two-day hike. So I listened to a counsel of mercy.

On the evening of Roswel's return, we all again met and mapped out the work for the following week. As we finished and began to compliment ourselves, we heard another announcement on the radio. A distant relative of Sohn Alpet had died. The funeral was to be held at an in-law's house in a section of Kitti deep in the hills. He was distressed at missing work. Covering his face, he said he would have to attend the funeral. Roger and I decided to go with him. "Oh no," he replied, "the path is not suitable for foreigners." But we prevailed, and he was right. The path was rocky, precipitous, and muddy, and we had to ford several streams. However, it led to our only good day's work in Wene. With everyone from that section gathered in one place for the funeral, we were able to complete the census of the entire area.

Two days later, another radio announcement, another funeral, more obligations. This time, Sohn Alpet told Roswel to pretend he had not heard it. We had work to do and were not going to suspend it once more.

It might seem that the Pohnpeian death rate was unusually high. During this time, our work was directly or indirectly affected by twelve funerals. A severe flu epidemic had hit newborns and old people hard. Pohnpeians call respiratory afflictions — colds, influenza, and upper respiratory tract infections — the "sickness of foreigners." They have little hereditary immunity to the diseases of Westerners. Furthermore, the ships that came into port brought contagion directly from other countries around the world. Sometimes after a ship had docked, a wave of sickness would pass through the island and then abate until the next ship arrived carrying a different set of germs.

Moreover, Pohnpeians simply have more relatives than most Westerners do. Kinship relationships extend over a broader base of people. They have reciprocal relationships with members of their mother's clan, their father's clan, their spouse's clan, people married into these groups, and relatives that the attenuated western kinship system has ignored. Funerals last a minimum of four days with the degree of participation determined by the closeness of the relationship. Some funerals last ten days. The extent of personal grief that a person feels is less important than the fact of kinship. Gifts of food or produce from the land are required. How large a contribution is also determined by the closeness of the relationship.

One part of life in Wene surprised me. The use of high language was constant. I still hoped that the forms Sohn Alpet taught me were only for the Paramount Chiefs (whom I devoutly planned to avoid). No sooner had we stepped off the boat than he began using high language to Roger and me. Our host and hostess used high language to us, to the Peace Corps couple, and in front of their children.

At every homestead, at every public gathering, and on the paths between, I heard styles of speech that were not covered in the classic anthropological articles by my colleagues. I heard people proud of their linguistic virtuosity, marking themselves off from others by the skills of their tongues. Sometimes I thought this was a game they played on each other and certainly on us because I could find no reason for the war of words. Yet, in this verbal chess or poker, they scored points by speaking of themselves with humility and modesty while exalting their opponents to absurd levels of status. This game, if indeed my view is correct, fits into the Pohnpeian personality of public modesty and private ambition. Life in Wene seemed to be a covert verbal competition.

Sohn Alpet continually warned us that the people of Wene had been spoiled by the Peace Corps presence. He claimed that they did not understand U.S. economic concepts. Their dilemma was how to live traditional lives without modern sources of income. The men could go into Kolonia to work and send money back. But the customary obligations, farming, and feasting that gave their lives meaning could not be sustained from such a distance. This also assumes that jobs were available for people without modern job skills and knowledge of English. Only 44 percent of the men from this area had wage-labor employment (compared to 85 percent in Kolonia).

The Peace Corps training center established several years earlier and the invasion of free-spending Americans had infused the area with cash and unrealistic expectations. In Wene, people were torn between their canons of hospitality to strangers and financial negotiations, the rules for which they had not learned in an ordinary market setting. They craved both economic reciprocity and economic power. At night, some of the men listened to the news on the radio, which reported the price of pork on the Chicago market. This figure, with approximately 10 percent added for sentimental value, would be quoted the next morning as the worth of the pigs they hoped to sell. Never mind that this pricing structure bore no relationship to the laws of supply and demand on remote islands. Arguments with each other over selling and buying pigs (as well as other deals, bargains, or bartering) were constant. With foreigners, the problems sometimes seemed insurmountable, and I dreaded pig negotiations in particular.

The community had no office jobs, no motor vehicles, no bars, no roads, no electricity, no running water, no restaurants, no tourist facilities of any kind. Wene did have a Catholic mission, a Protestant church, a tiny dispensary and a school that went up to the eighth grade. Copra was a major source of income. This dried coconut meat is harvested all over the Pacific, then bagged and shipped to the Philippines for processing. But the development of a host of better substitutes for the rich oils and residues of copra have reduced this source of income, and the world price for copra has fallen. On Pohnpei, which has a poor climate for drying copra, income from copra averaged only about $250 per harvester per year. Despite these limitations, the homesteads in Wene were large, lovely, and proudly maintained.

The other major competition was in the ancient and arcane rivalries between municipalities. The neighboring municipality of Madolenihmw is ranked higher than Kitti. Small differences in feasting customs between the municipalities, the order of the kava poundings, and the timing for the opening of the earth oven, are raised to intense levels of concern and comment. In the past, the men of Kitti and Madolenihmw went to battle against each other. Now they compete in prestige marriages and in correct interpretations of history and custom.

Furthermore, the people of Wene have asserted a historic primacy and cultural superiority over the rest of Kitti. The retelling of the legends that back the storytellers' side becomes another competitive use of language. After listening to these discussions among both Pohnpeians and U.S. colleagues, I think that they also compete with others in convincing anthropologists that their separate regional views of history should be ratified.

The community of Wene has deep historical roots and what most acknowledge as the most intense traditionalism anywhere in Pohnpei. These people pride themselves on strict adherence to *tiaken sapw,* the customs of the land, a phrase which they use much like the U.S. concept of the law of the land. As long as money is not the topic of conversation, they are cooperative and proud of their skills and their heritage.

The four of us were distressed by our failures in bargaining. As Roger wryly commented, "We were strangers and they took us in." Agreements on which we shook hands fell through, and written contracts were subject to further haggling. The funerals, financial problems, and the sicknesses we suffered during this visit cut into the amount of work we had hoped to achieve. I was apprehensive about the difficulties of fielding and financing the medical team later in the year. We would have to negotiate every detail of housing, food, laundry, transportation, and other services necessary to sustain a dozen people for a month.

We decided to cut our stay short and return to celebrate Christmas Day in Kolonia. As Roswel attached the outboard motor to the whaleboat, Sohn Alpet stood erect at the helm and pronounced in a perfect imitation of John Wayne's cowboy English "I sho' will be happy to shake the dust of this goldarn place off my boots." That is the only English I ever heard him speak.

In the month following the working trip to Wene, I had nagging colds and a feeling of despondency. The project's work had not gone well. I worried about the accuracy of the census and the hidden frictions that we encountered.

One ordinary morning, Sohn Alpet came by as usual to discuss the day's work and the Kolonia census. We talked about the feasts in Wene, and he explained aspects of the feasting system to me. Casually, he announced that my knowledge of the intricacies of a feast should be expanded. Therefore, he and his family had decided to stage a demonstration to include the appropriate foods, their preparation, the earth oven, speech-making, and above all, the proper manners. He set a date, gave me a list of instructions, and departed. What a good teaching tool, I thought, similar to his tactfulness in making me learn respect language.

Our feast house had a newly thatched roof that had not been dedicated — another reason for a feast. I took the money for the pig out of my personal budget, rather than the U.S. government's pig budget. Sohn Alpet negotiated its purchase without strain and tethered it in the yard for several days.

On the appointed day, his wife and daughters arrived with wash basins of blossoms to make flower headdresses. Ioannes installed a special stick for husking the coconuts and dispatched some young boys up the coconut and breadfruit trees for leaves and fruit. Akina made irreverent jokes while she helped with the food. Sohn Alpet arrived with yams and a kava plant. The women sat quietly on the gnarled roots of the breadfruit trees and wove their headdresses. Relaxed, they pulled the tops of their dresses down to their waists. When they realized that I had no traditional cups in which to serve kava, they picked up a thick piece of green Coke-bottle glass and began to scrape the halves of a coconut shell. Under their firm hands, the rich, walnut brown of a kava cup began to emerge. They laughed as I insisted on cleaning the kava stone thoroughly. Pwutak, the dog, had marked his territory.

The men built a fire over the rocks and below the eaves of thatch at the wide entrance of the little feast house. Then they grabbed the pig and stuck a knife in its throat; Sohn Alpet eyed me covertly to test my threshold of squeamishness. The pig squealed, bled, and died. They removed the internal organs and singed its skin by dragging it across the hot coals. It rested on leaves with the breadfruit and yams. The elements of a traditional feast were now in order.

Spreading out the hot coals and glowing rocks out with wooden tongs, they laid the yams and breadfruit in the oven first, then the splayed pig. The men covered the food with broad leaves and anchored the edges of the oven with rocks. Wisps of smoke, which gave a rich flavor to the food, escaped through the leaves. Watching this, I was aware of how old and widespread these customs were. Throughout the entire Pacific were cultures that shared the same words and tools to make the earth oven. From Hawaii to the highlands of New Guinea, ancient cultures prepare and eat the steamed vegetables and meat or fish. When the steam from the earth oven began to rise, the men prepared to pound kava.

Throughout these preparations, Sohn Alpet kept up his running commentary. He explained what they were doing and why it accorded with tradition. He emphasized the proper manners to be observed even in a small family feast. He seated us carefully on the platform of the feast house and gave orders to open the earth oven, distribute the food, and serve the kava. Then he made a simple speech emphasizing (I thought) points of etiquette and the history of our research project. He remarked on the classic Pohnpeian values of cooperation, humility, hard work, and respect to the high-titled people and elders.

I learned much and, thanks to Sohn Alpet, would be comfortable with feasting formalities. I accepted his explanations at face value and thought little more about the feast. The project entered a new and invigorating phase. We were working hard with language lessons, and my lassitude and colds disappeared. But weeks later, I began to hear comments about what happened at the little feast. I do not know when these references began to form a pattern or even when my western consciousness admitted another reality.

According to the low-keyed gossip, Sohn Alpet had staged the feast to lift the curses to which we had fallen prey in Wene. To him, the evidence was strong. We had more problems than bad luck alone could explain. Perhaps germs do cause colds or flu, but why to that particular person at that time? It was the project people who became sick, not the people of Wene.

He never claimed, to me at least, that a sorcerer had put a spell on us or added something in our food to make us confused and sick. These are the classic methods of sorcerers in many parts of the world, including Pohnpei before the enlightenment. But he mentioned from time to time that feeling jealousy or greed toward others was the same as sending a curse. By harboring such feelings, you wished them evil and rejoiced in their bad fortune. The project would have been harmed had he brought specific accusations of sorcery. In any case, he was too good a Christian to engage in a war of spells. Instead, he planned the feast and quietly passed the word that our troubles were over. Let others draw conclusions.

Sorcery is a matter of anxiety and secretiveness. In a society that places the value of cooperation above all others, sorcery is competition and rivalry unleashed. It is said that sorcerers in the past had the power to send killing magic. The only way to cure this lethal curse was more powerful magic sent back on the head of the sorcerer. If, in fact, sorcery exists, the most common form is for a sorcerer to place a magical substance in food, drink, or bathing places or to send forth magical spells of harm. Public gatherings can be dangerous. This is one reason why little food is consumed at feasts. Sometimes the practice may misfire like a poorly loaded gun and rebound against the sorcerer or even injure the innocent. Naturally, sorcerers or their clients cannot brag about their successes or complain about their failures.

Initially, Pohnpeians will deny the contemporary existence of such practices. But sorcery fears feed on hidden rivalries, individual charisma, and a need to explain sudden sickness, death, or terrible accidents where no ordinary explanations suffice. The fears persist, and reasoning gives no answers. In Pohnpei, as in all human societies, there are dreadful events that require an explanation. Westerners may say these are coincidence, bad luck, the way things are, God's will, or poor planning. That the evil thoughts of others have the power to hurt and kill is an elegant belief system that continues to have strong explanatory power in many societies.

By no scientific standards in western logic can I prove that we fell victim to sorcery. I have no evidence that anyone spiked our food or sent spells of misfortune upon us. Nonetheless, on some level, I came to believe in the power of jealousy, fear, competitiveness, and greed to cause illness and bad luck. The quiet conviction of the Pohnpeians that the explanatory models of western science and Christianity were inadequate to account for all human feelings and events sifted through my consciousness.

Little things happened in Wene. I stepped on more of those repulsive toads than during all the rest of my time on Pohnpei. My feet were continually covered with pig dung and scratches. Ordinary objects were lost, then mysteriously found. Precious flashlight batteries refused to operate during those weeks. The mail was mislaid. We had strange dreams. It was not only the illnesses and frustrations of work.

The question of sorcery came up obliquely throughout our stay on the island. If we were sorcerized, then the curses were lifted by no deeds or counterspells that I witnessed, but by a spirit of cooperation and mutual respect at the little feast. The petty sicknesses and malaise never returned.

Late one night, Michael, the only U.S. doctor at the district hospital, drove up to the house, disheveled and frantic. A newborn baby had a birth defect that required immediate surgery. But the baby's parents refused to sign the permissions. If they did not sign within a few days, the baby would die. Since the infant was in Sohn Alpet's extended family, Michael thought we could help. I went to the hospital to learn that a radio call for relatives had already gone out.

Through the following day and into that night, the family met and talked. In their view, the hospital had told them what was wrong with the baby, but not why. They trusted western medicine to correct the defect through surgery. But such action would not solve the real problem. Unless they themselves, out of the traditions of Pohnpeian medicine, determined the cause of the sickness, the baby would later fall victim to it, or indeed, would not survive the operation. A Pohnpeian illness had a Pohnpeian cause and cure. Such causes could include sorcery against some less-innocent family member that had ricocheted onto the baby. Perhaps an evil spirit had caused the illness. If a study of the symptoms revealed that cause, the spirit could be placated and sent away. Alternatively, unresolved frictions, jealousies, or arguments within the larger family network may have caused this. The families' consensus about causation was required before the surgery could be attempted.

They consulted curers, both inside and outside the hospital. They found no evidence for sorcery nor spirit-caused illnesses; family frictions were apparently the root of the problem. In a process similar to group dynamics or family therapy in the West, the relatives began to speak about their actions and those of others that could have brought harm. Pressured by time and their love for the infant, they gave voice to their hurts, the petty recriminations of the past, and their continuing disagreements.

In these nonstop discussions, several key conflicts became apparent. The failure to solve an argument stemming from a marriage contract and land dispute between two families had festered. The parties to the dispute had been gossiping about each other and had permitted hard feelings to prevent their participation in feasting and other traditional responsibilities of the extended family. It was the ill will they bore each other that had been deflected onto the infant, an innocent hostage to their conflicts.

This, then, was the cause. The cure was to renegotiate the dispute. Like skilled labor-management consultants or divorce mediators, they hammered out a new contract that addressed the accusations of all sides. People's private feelings were neither revealed nor soothed. The agreement meant that they would forgive, forget, and cooperate with each other in public. Only this would save the baby's life. Exhausted but quietly relieved, they signed the permission to operate. The time had come for Christian prayers and western medicine.

The baby lived and thrived.

The Pohnpeian treatment of illness involves the body and soul of the patient, as well as the social configurations surrounding the patient. Hospital (western) medicines were often criticized as insensitive to the psychological dimensions of illness. Nonetheless, the western cures are enthusiastically used while supplemented by native curing practices. For example, hundreds of plant species are used in Pohnpeian recipes or therapies that are carefully handed down to specialists in diagnosis and treatment. Western medicine was simply grafted onto this extensive curing system. In fact, western medicine was often the only cure for the diseases brought by Westerners.

I had excellent results from consulting Pohnpeian medical specialists. Sometimes now, I wish for a consultation and one of their cures. Occasionally, I even think of the advantages of putting a sorcery curse on someone, although that is a base yearning. Roger was clever and regularly sent me to curers so he could find out what they did and how they did it. I was examined; I drank several potions reputed to cure one minor condition or another. I was a guinea pig for science.

One steamy day, Roger roared up to our homestead on the motorbike. He had been collecting traditional medical practices from a renowned curer whom I called "the Pagan." Unlike other men of his generation, the Pagan did not preface his remarks with pious statements about being a good Christian and renouncing the evil past. The Pagan offered Roger a splendid deal.

"He claims that he can give me a magical spell that will guarantee the complete obedience of my wife for one year," Roger announced gleefully. "Only ninety dollars!"

I laughed. "It would take a lot more money than that, and how do you know it will work?" I had no intention of paying for my own obedience training and no desire to find out the spell's effect.

But Roger and the Pagan had not given up. Another offer followed the next week.

"What about the same magical spell for six months and forty-five dollars?" Roger asked on behalf of the Pagan. But I still did not wish to be bewitched into docility.

Finally, Roger reported the last offer. "We will split the money and the results with Pedro and Kioko [the couple with whom we had lived]. Pedro knows this will work, and he needs it even more than I do. This will buy at least partial obedience from our wives." I happened to believe that the charm would not work unless Kioko and I agreed. Perhaps the combination of the power of suggestion with a financial investment would have activated the charm. I still wonder if the Pagan's last offer was a cheap spell without my consent.

Sorcery and magic are not invariably negative forces. Besides the kind of powers that hurt and kill people, there are powers that create good feelings. Many of these originate in the leaves of plants and in the power of language through spells or chants. Ways of expelling bad medicine and sending back destruction are counter-curses. The ability to create or to stop quarrels was called "causing to drift." My favorite was "making the inside well," which means to bring peace and comfort to the grieving. The powers of consolation and peace would indeed be a gift of the spirit to a troubled person or a worried community.

On one of our boat trips, I asked Sohn Alpet what Pohnpeians thought about Americans. "Americans are very clever and very energetic. You have invented so many things." He elaborated on the space program, machines, cars, airplanes, outboard motors, and other items of technology. "Your political system is very strange. You have high chiefs and men of wisdom like President Kennedy and Martin Luther King, but they are killed for it. Even in pagan times, we did not behave like that. I hear that you put men in jail for helping their brothers-in-law. Why should men go to jail for doing their duty to help their relatives? What will your sisters do if their husbands are in trouble?"

I explained how nepotism and favoritism in awarding contracts and jobs undermined our economic system. But I did not understand why our leaders were killed.

"It is good for us to know more Americans," he continued. "Your government was wise to send the Peace Corps, economic development people, and our research project, which will help people in the world. But all of you have one major problem. You smell funny and your feet are dirty."

"What?" I demanded. "It is people in other places who smell funny." I was insulted. Like other Americans, I was prepared to be criticized about my country's foreign policy, President Nixon, and the war in Southeast Asia, but Americans spend millions of dollars on soaps, perfumes, and preparations to cleanse the body and to disguise basic human odors. I had never heard of another culture in history so obsessed with cleanliness.

"Then that is the reason why you smell funny," he retorted. "Moreover, Americans do not know how to walk with zories in mud and dust without getting dirty. No matter what they do, their feet are always dirty." As I contrived to hide my admittedly dirty feet, I realized how relative smell and dirt must be, except within one's own culture where these standards are absolute. I began to look at feet and, to be sure, Americans' feet were stained by the omnipresent mud and the minerals of the volcanic soils while the Micronesians' feet were not. Although I vowed to scrub my feet with the hard brushes the Pohnpeians used, they never looked clean again.

Pohnpeians regularly initiated conversations about themselves and Americans. They continually questioned me about customs and would return the favor with lectures on what they thought I should know about themselves. Because the research questionnaire was attempting to reveal how Pohnpeians felt about their own lives and the stresses they perceived, I listened to how they talked about these problems. When we discussed their feelings or when I asked the endless questions anthropologists always ask, I often received answers that bore scant relationship to the questions. Perhaps I asked about a particular place, a story about one of the clans, or the quality of kinship relations. The answers came frequently in the form of myths or stories, the favorite of which was a long, involved tale about a cultural hero named Lord Kelekel.

Parts of this tale are often told separately. The story has been superbly analyzed by other generations of anthropologists, so I had small interest in collecting yet another version. But I was fascinated by how easily the stories crept into ordinary conversations, kava poundings, and public discussions. I did not then recognize that the answers are in the story. These are not just tales told to children. They encode some of the deeper meanings that Pohnpeians ascribe to their common history.

The story of Lord Kelekel begins some time in the past (once upon a time), when a dynasty of ruthless men called the Lords of Deleur lived in the great city of Nan Madol and ruled over the island.

> The great gods had doomed the Lord of Deleur. The titled men of Pohnpei felt no sympathy for him because of his cruelty and oppression. He did as he wished and did not respect the high gods. It is claimed that he summoned people to his presence and ate them. It is even said that he required his subjects to bring him their head lice, which he enjoyed eating. He even imprisoned the mighty God of Thunder, Nansapwe, who contrived to escape.

> The God of Thunder went upwind to Katau to visit his clanswoman. On the way his royal canoe sank, but a sea bass magically turned a taro flower into a needle fish, who saved the God of Thunder. He gave her a sour fruit to eat and she became pregnant. She bore a son who was called Lord Kelekel.

> Eventually, Lord Kelekel grew up and gathered together his resources and supporters (who numbered 333 fighting men and assorted women and children) to stage an invasion of Pohnpei. They sailed off, but mistaking the palm trees for tall people, they retreated. They sailed downwind to the atoll of Ant near Pohnpei. There the Chief gave them 333 baskets of breadfruit seeds. He taught them to speak the language and to know the customs of Pohnpei.

> After this, they launched their fleet peacefully into a harbor in Madolenihmw. Lord Kelekel was extremely clever. His supporters took beautiful young women as wives. But he picked an old servant woman from whom he learned the food habits, work, geography, and customs of the island. He did not reveal his true status as a leader to the Lords of Deleur or any Pohnpeians.

War broke out when the children of the two groups began fighting among themselves. The troops of Lord Kelekel were outnumbered and began to retreat when a brave man, of his own free will, speared his foot to the ground and refused to retreat. The invader troops rallied and won the battle. The Lord of Deleur fell into a river and lives there today as a fish.

Many other stories about the exploits of the hero, magical creatures, spirits, and the cruelties of the Lords are woven into this basic framework. The moral of the story changes from time to time. Sometimes they said that after this, Pohnpei changed and became peaceful. People valued hard work and quarreled less with each other. The successful resistance to tyranny brought a new order of peace comparable to the American struggles for independence and freedom. Sometimes they cite stories to support customs, such as respect for high people and elders. The stories in the myth cycle of Lord Kelekel seem to give answers to such questions as: what kind of people are we, why do we act and feel the way we do, what is really important to us? Because the answers are indirect, it took me a long time to accept the levels of meaning offered in the stories.

Sometimes, answers to questions I had not asked came in the form of sayings tidbits of verbal wisdom and metaphors. English speakers say: "a stitch in time saves nine," "don't sweat the small stuff," or "don't throw me in that briar patch." Pohnpeians say: "See, this is like water running under boulders. You can hear the water, but you can not see it. You can complain about the actions of high people or the American administration, but nothing will come of it. They will still be doing the same thing tomorrow. The thoughts of others flow silently." The water continues to run quietly under the boulders. The fears of sorcery persist and cannot be dammed by the rocks of reason. The quiet undercurrents of life continue.

Letters from the field:

Dearest Ones,

The MILI ship came last Friday with the lumber we need to build a door to the kitchen, and the carpenters were scheduled for Saturday. Alas, too late. After all the precautions we take when we leave the house with its meager belongings, we were robbed while we slept. They (or he) poked a hole in the screen. Sohn Alpet, Akina, and Ioannis were terribly upset because they thought the police would suspect them. But I cleared that up in another memorable trip to the constabulary.

About three times a week, at night, we have visitors who peer through the windows and through the cracks in the walls. That is how often we hear them; the quieter ones may come more often. Pete Hill, who is director for Community Action (whatever that is), says we must accept the fairness of reverse anthropology. After all, they are curious about Americans and we are the only ones living in the area. Now we are installing wire safety screens on all the so-called windows. I am making curtains by hand. That should solve the problem of peepers.

We can't move the kerosene freezer out of the so-called bedroom until we fix the timbers in the kitchen floor. We can't do that without redoing the door. But all the two-by-fours or two-by-sixes in town are sitting out in the lagoon, waiting to be unloaded. Another ship is tied up at the only dock. They are behind schedule because Friday is payday, and everything in Kolonia stops for two days while people go to bars, kava poundings, shopping, or to feasts. Apparently no financial inducement will convince stevedores to work around the clock, and the ships do not schedule their arrivals.

Kolonia is temporarily out of sugar, and the donuts taste worse than ever. There must be some hoarding because a very nice clerk at Carlos' store slipped me some from the back.

Public Works has taken a benevolent interest in the house. They raised the shower head from three feet to six feet off the ground. They know that foreigners shower standing up rather than sitting down (although I'm flexible). Now they are going to install an outdoor light, as it is widely gossiped that the nocturnal peeping has not abated in the least. I offered to pay the city for these services, but the workmen assured me that would be impossible because their record-keeping system is in hopeless confusion.

Akina, our language instructor, has worked for the Peace Corps in the same job and knows the methods. She is full of local gossip. She is an entrepreneur who supports her six children by operating a beer parlor and a bingo (pronounced pinko) game. She says people are pinko-mad and don't want to stop until dawn. Competitors pay a nickel a card to play; the winner gets the pot, and our language teacher gets 10 percent. A small-time Las Vegas! Four of her kids are adopted and several are doing well at college in Hawaii (courtesy of pinko). One of her daughters gave birth to triplets, identical little girls. That is rare in these kinds of societies. Triple trouble and they are just adorable. Akina tells outrageous dirty jokes in Pohnpeian. High-ranking Pohnpeian men don't approve of her free-wheeling ways.

Our menagerie of animals is endearing. They work for a living and for this are rewarded with leftover rice and mackerel. We eat chicken several times a week because it's cheap and usually available from the last boat. The two cats and the dog line up beside us on the floor and wait their turns for the bones.

Dear Len and our Chapel Hill friends,

Public health is more than diet and heart disease. It is toilets, too. But adopting toilets as good sanitation has a long way to go here.

Last week I ran into a Peace Corps volunteer while on a hike into Nett. Who else would have a roll of toilet paper under one arm and a jar of peanut butter under the other? We chatted and shared a drinking coconut. He had just spent two years out in the wilds of Kitti working in what is euphemistically called community development. He was supposed to work with the community on public health issues (translated, build water seal toilets). With heroic effort, he had succeeded in convincing two families to build the toilets.

His theory for the reluctance of islanders to construct the toilets is the price of toilet paper. Traditionally, they used leaves, which are abundant and cost nothing. Leaves, however soft, do not flush down the water seal toilet, and toilet paper, assuming it is available, is expensive relative to the incomes in some of the remote areas. We discussed the public health problems created by poor sanitation and the virtues the water seal toilet. He is depressed at the failure of his efforts. We speculated about the kinds of people who, with the best of intentions, design projects for the undeveloped world but who have never examined fundamental assumptions about their own world.

Jack wrote us that at your last meeting in Chapel Hill, you all discussed sending Jones' wayward son out here to take photographs. I realize that Jones Senior is famous, but spending that kind of money ought to have some value for anthropology and medical research. Roger and I remain dubious. As far as public relations goes, we are really opposed. Taking pictures to hand out is what shyster lawyers do in New Orleans to impress their poor black clients.

We have to justify to confused or cynical critics daily why this project should be conducted. This is particularly crucial in regard to the hospital. They are understaffed, underequipped, and cannot cope with the volume of patients. Any extra money needs to go for public welfare via the hospital. Ian's dynamic personality has led them to think that we are going to help with these problems. If you check my notes of his visit, you will see just what he promised—not much.

The Pohnpeians are genuinely cordial people who will cooperate with us if we act honorably (as we are doing). They do not need gimmicks. One of our jobs here is public relations, and I do not want to be saddled with a snake oil salesman or a kid on a junket who knows nothing about culture relativity, research, or Micronesia. Next we will be passing out key chains!

I am hoping that you or Pat (another anthropologist would be useful) can come out here when the medical team arrives. Jack agrees with us, but he is too modest to tell you that it is the extraordinary respect he enjoys here that has opened so many doors for us.

I appreciate your sending me the Maidenform bra. Where did you ever find a red one with heavy stitched cups?

Menlau and kalahngan (that means thanks for everything).

- 4 -

Smoke Follows the
High People

We were seated in the centre of the canoe house, upon mats; and yams, breadfruit, plantains, fish, bits of cold game of some sort, the class of which we could not at first decide, were brought to us. The building was filled in every chink by natives, seated, the men with crossed legs, like Turks, and the women on their heels. . . . Parties of two or three would come down to where we sat, walking with their bodies bent almost double. They took hold of our persons very familiarly, women and men, and gave frequent clucks of admiration at the blue veins which were marked through our skins, on parts of the body which had not been usually exposed to be bronzed by the sun. My comrades feared the Indians were Cannibals, and this examination was to discover whether we were in good roasting case.
—From the 1826 diary of a shipwrecked sailor, James O'Connell

S ohn Alpet called out, "Hello there, empty nest," as he approached our homestead one muggy Sunday afternoon. When I heard the polite, respectful form of greeting used when one is not certain who is inside a house, I knew something was going to happen. As he added other honorifics, a rare compliment, and a promise to tell me the incest story he had sworn never to reveal, I grew more curious about his visit.

The more earnest was his purpose, the longer he took to reach his point. On this occasion, he had a financial proposal, so the conversation was particularly circuitous. He wanted an outboard motor for the boat he was building. He and his family commuted regularly between their homes in Madolenihmw and Kolonia. Overland travel was impossible. Owning a boat and outboard motor was both necessity and personal prestige.

Sohn Alpet had anticipated our budgetary dilemmas. The government grant was generous but severely restricted by category. We could rent all the boats we needed to complete the project, but on a research grant, we could not purchase a boat, much less an outboard motor. He proposed the solution: we would loan him the money for the outboard and he would repay the loan by renting the boat, motor, and drivers back to us. It was an extremely sensible proposal and we wrote out a contract. Ironically, this solution saved the government a great deal of money in the travel category; we returned the excess at the end of the granting period.

Extremely proud of his new possession, he carried it himself and wiped off specks of mud. An acquisition of this magnitude had to be christened and the contract ratified in traditional fashion. He and his extended family staged a lovely dinner in the feast house with yams (fried, baked, and cooked with coconut cream), taro done in the same manner, fried pork, cucumber salad, mangrove crabs, and other delicacies. We invited everyone who had worked on the project.

Sohn Alpet stood up to deliver the appropriate speech and announced that by this action I had adopted him as a son. Henceforth he would address me as his mother. Never mind that my son was a generation older than me. I understood fully. Had he announced that I was an adopted daughter, I would have felt better. Many of the Peace Corps members prided themselves on being children of the family with whom they lived. But children have less responsibility than parents. Mothers take care of their sons. Because he had a real mother in her nineties and a number of aunts whom he addressed as mother, this meant only one kind of responsibility. I would have financial and feasting obligations to his extended family far in excess of the filial duties a fictive daughter owed.

I could not, even tactfully, disavow this honor in public, so I asked what kinship relationship this new outboard motor had. The family laughed and decided that it, too, was my son. I could assign its elder brother to care for it. The family was openly pleased and instructed me to avoid eating eels, the taboo food of the Lasialap clan.

Privately, I worried that Sohn Alpet had more tricks up his sleeve. Although I regularly received offers to adopt babies, this was the first time I had been assigned a family status. I also suspected that some Pohnpeians had exploited fictive relationships and manipulated foreigners with them. For a brief moment, I wondered why Roger was singularly excluded from this honor. Did Sohn Alpet recognize that I was in charge of the household and project budgets?

Fortunately, a flash of anthropological insight replaced my suspicions. I had just become a mother in a matrilineal society. The rules of kinship are: first, mothers and sons always belong to the same clan, and second, you never marry anyone who belongs to your clan. Ergo, Roger was just an in-law from another clan. Sons take their status from their mother. High-ranking mothers pass on subtle benefits to their sons. Sohn Alpet was a clever man. He was paying me a compliment, thanking me for the boat deal, giving me a useful new status, and piggy-backing on my status. No wonder he extolled my virtues and the worth of the project in his public speeches.

With the troubled trip to Wene behind us and a new outboard motor for easy traveling, we scheduled visits to other districts to work on the organization of and census for the blood pressure research, as well as our other ethnographic projects. Living in one area alone, such as Kolonia, gave a limited, even distorted, picture of Pohnpeian life. In town, we had less interaction with family life and the intricacies of a tightly knit community. For these reasons, we chose to live for a time in an area of Madolenihmw near Sohn Alpet's homestead.

The frictions and economic stress that so marked Wene seemed muted, even absent in the hilly area of Wapar. The work of the census was effortless and easy friendships with people in the community made immersion in the daily routines a pleasure. Instead of funerals, we attended a series of feasts to honor weddings, new titles, trips abroad, and the yearly obligations of the section to its titled leaders. Most of the children and adults used our first names. I heard little or no high language spoken, although the people of the area were extremely conscientious about respecting customs and their duties to the Paramount Chief.

Our host, with whom financial arrangements had been straightforward, laughed easily and, with friendly grace, enjoyed the presence of foreign anthropologists. Souehdi and his wife had nine children. But the number of children in the household never added up to nine. One daughter had been adopted by Souehdi's eldest sister, who was wife of the Paramount Chief of U. Two sons were doing well at school, and another lived on and off with his paternal grandmother who needed help on her homestead. A perky little girl about eight years old was actually a distant relative who had come for dinner several years earlier and never left. Other children dropped in to play with the chubby, cheerful baby of the household who was never out of someone's arms. Various of these children stayed for days or weeks.

I felt very comfortable in the atmosphere of this household. I planned to talk to women about their lives. But my anthropological training up to that time had given me few theories, questions, or methods to study women except as adjunct to the lives of men and children. When I asked questions, I received stock answers: "You should ask my husband about that," or "men know about things like that." "I'm baking bread; come and watch." "I wash clothes; let's go to the river." Frequently I heard, "That question reminds me of a story about Lord Kelekel. It's a good one." The women gossiped and talked about their children, but they did not regard their lives or opinions as significant. Perhaps my job and my childlessness gave me more of a masculine status than a feminine one.

On the other hand, their unguarded friendliness made it easy to follow the rhythm of their days. Women are expected to work less arduously than men. They say, "But that is just how women are." I thought of cultures where the incessant labor of women ages and kills them prematurely and people say, "Of course, that is just how women are."

Every occasion was social. At the bathing pool, a short walk down a path from the homestead, pigs and a water buffalo wallowed in the muddy side. On the clear-water side, I bathed to the giggles of little girls who had never seen foreign ladies bathe. "Naughty, naughty," they whispered as they clutched each other for support. Naughty was not in reference to their behavior in spying on my ablutions, but to my awkward use of the bathing slip, my inexperience in handling water buffalo, and my acceptance of young male observers in four nearby coconut trees.

We rose before 6:00 each morning to the sounds of children raking the yard. In addition to the main three-room house that was too hot to use in the daytime, the family had a large feast and a small feast house, a cooking house, and a sick house built for a relative who had been lovingly cared for until his recent death. Near the cook house was a copra drying shed (also suitable for drying clothes in the rain). On the path leading to the Protestant church was a small store and another small tin building. A rocky path led to the spring used for bathing, washing, and collecting water for cooking. On the edge of the uncleared woods were outhouses and on the opposite side, the decorated graves of family members.

During the day, Roger and I either sat in the feast house as men came to visit and talk or we made calls in the neighborhood. It was amazing to live with so many children who took seriously the saying, "kids should be seen and not heard." The children did not interrupt the adults or cause the disturbances that mark most western households with even one child underfoot. They did not ask questions nor vie for attention. I saw this behavior many times. Although children are a constant presence at all occasions, they are not disruptive. Neither, however, will they converse with or answer questions from adults. Night and day, they followed me and watched my actions. But it was almost impossible to talk to them since respect for elders is so deeply engrained.

I was careful not to touch the children's heads. In Polynesian and Micronesian societies, particularly in Pohnpei, the head is vulnerable because power can flow from high people into those of lower status and injure them. It was difficult to remember this taboo. For most Westerners, I suspect, this is a normal gesture of affection or patronage. But in Pohnpei, one does not raise heads symbolically above one's betters nor expose children to a negative flow of power.

One evening after a delicious supper of freshly caught lagoon fish, we sat in the light of a kerosene lantern as the children dropped off to sleep one by one. Relaxed after a good day's work, I paid only casual attention to the conversation. Suddenly, I heard Souehdi making plans to restructure my life. "I think my plan will work well. You will take one of the boys back to America with you. I promise you that he will work very hard in school." He had decided that one of his bright sons should attend school in the United States courtesy of his newly adopted mother, who would provide opportunities for advancement. My mind flashed on the cost of higher education and occasional trips to the Trust Territory to maintain the bonds of friendship and family. I tried to imagine a sexually precocious Micronesian teenager following the custom of night-crawling in a New Orleans middle school. I gently declined another opportunity for Micronesian parenthood.

Some imagine that people in the tropics take advantage of the sun-softened days to nap every afternoon. True elsewhere, perhaps, but not in Pohnpei. Souehdi, like other men of his generation, worked very hard. I followed him through two weeks of activities. On Saturday, he organized a *kamadipw en mwomwodiso,* a feast by a church congregation in the presence of the Paramount Chief. This meant harvesting his own foodstuffs from his concealed gardens and organizing relatives and neighbors to work. Sunday was the church service in which he acted as lay minister, then the feast for which he was responsible, then a family meeting at his feast house. On Monday, he went to work at the District Office, where he was secretary and treasurer. This work provided him with a boat and motor and a small salary.

Tuesday, he paid taxes. That is, he donated his labor to the Paramount Chief of Madolenihmw to work on the construction of the new district feast house. Everyone was required to contribute what they had to give: money, labor, supplies, or food to feed the workers. Wednesday, he worked long hours on his own homestead, his gardens, and the tiny store in his front yard. Thursday, he went to Kolonia for the day, to do business for the church, shop for his family and store, and represent his district at a meeting. All day Friday, he made preparations for his daughter's wedding. Saturday, he held the wedding, and we feasted all day. Sunday was church again, a little rest, and a big family organizational meeting. Monday, he gathered the useful adolescent males and females in his extended family to build a new house for his mother. Everyone worked in the manner of barn raising on the American frontier, and by nightfall she moved in. The following days brought more activity as the weekend's feasting demands drew closer.

Souehdi's work ethic had a purpose. He had a high title that was above his station, that is, beyond what his clan affiliation, birth order, or family connections would ordinarily entitle him. His relatively high title was a recognition of his zeal in working for the Paramount Chief, the church, the clan, and the general good of the community. Some people are born into the nobility. Others achieve it through hard work and success.

A very sick old man in Souehdi's clan had a very high title. The Paramount Chief of Madolenihmw promised this title to Souehdi, who could not routinely aspire to such heights, because of his industry on behalf of the district feast house. The Paramount Chief had been displeased on occasions when food was not provided to the laborers. Souehdi organized his family to serve pigs, yams, and other foods on a huge scale. Thus it was expected that at the memorial feast for the old man with the very high title, the Chief would confer the vacant title on his loyal subject. Everyone also knew that Souehdi would speak modestly, "This title should belong to my clan seniors; I am unworthy." But the High Chief would persist, and finally, Souehdi would claim the rewards of hard endeavor.

Sometimes men had difficulty finding a path to achievement or economic stability. Josep, one of the teachers in the elementary school, was a good example of the pull between modern ways, which involved additional education and personal ambition, and the traditional ways of family-centered mobility. A sizable portion of Josep's salary went to his extended family for feasts and other obligations. In addition, he worked for them several days a week, including weekdays. Part of Souehdi's personal achievement came from enlisting the money and labor of relatives such as Josep. In return for such help, a highstatus relative can pull others up behind him.

But Josep was ambivalent about striving for status and the rewards of the traditional systems. As he said, "If I have a title or not, it does not matter. One night at 11:00 the Paramount Chief gave me a title but I left to go home. I didn't care. The next morning at 5:00 my fathers [his father, adopted father and uncles] killed a pig for the Chief. I wasn't even present. They were worried about me and my status, so they made the title payment for me to avoid their own embarrassment."

His fondest ambition was to attend trade school in the United States. Although he taught English, he admitted his feelings of inadequacy in speaking it and his lack of familiarity with U.S. educational systems. He had tried to save money, but within a two week period, he gave more than 50 percent of his salary for his cousin's wedding, the District feast house of the Paramount Chief, and for the purchase of two pigs for two feasts. Moreover, he had donated his labor on both weekends and two school days. Although he expressed disaffection with the system that forced him to give so much of his earnings and time while the glory went to older male relatives, he was more and more an active participant in traditional affairs and made no effort to disengage himself.

He married young to an even younger woman after she bore a child. The pressures of tradition and modern education make marriage a subsidiary issue for him. Although he was one of many children, he was adopted into another family and thus expected to inherit some land. The Pohnpeian system of raising young people is seductive. They are drawn gradually into marriage, titles (even disavowed), land ownership, and the reflected power of the elders. At the same time, men of Josep's generation, trained in the individualistic ethic of the U.S. school systems, wanted to achieve success in the modern sector and earn good salaries. From my point of view, they had hard choices. The research question was how the work, the choices, the networks, the individualism, and the combinations affected their health and cardiovascular systems.

At church one morning, I was surprised to hear Josep pray in English. Because he was uncomfortable in English in general and in prayer in particular, I asked why he did that. "I couldn't get out of it, and I could absolutely not pray publicly in Pohnpeian because I don't know enough high language. God is higher than the Paramount Chiefs and must be addressed that way."

Later that week, we attended the section feast that is the annual obligation of all the high-ranking families in the geographical area to their Paramount Chief. In Madolenihmw, the emphasis seemed to be on hard work, proper contributions, and the spirit of traditions, rather than on the letter of the law, as was the case in Kitti. I heard more talk of yams, pit breadfruit, earth ovens, and community spirit than I did of minute features of etiquette, high language, or the failures of ancient customs. Had I spent the rest of my life on that island, I would still not have mastered all the technicalities concerning which titled person of which clan and/or subclan brought what and sat where at which feasts. Each of the five municipalities has subtle variations and each anthropologist who has worked there and each high-titled person with advancement strategies has special interpretations beyond the rules.

The Pohnpeians worried about creeping modernism taking over and destroying their customs. A new wrinkle of consumerism at the feasts symbolized their worries. The raised fronts of feast houses were filled with enameled wash basins (also called "iron pots"), which were filled with cooked rice, taro, cans of mackerel and corned beef, loaves of bread with suckers stuck in them, soy sauce bottles filled with pig fat, whole cooked chickens, and lengths of cloth or short-sleeved shirts. The expense in contributing these was said to be draining many families.

The unspoken rule for contributing these basins is similar to a potluck supper. Each group sponsoring the feast (family, congregation, geographical section) had to contribute enough for the high people, adults, and children. Through a complex redistribution system, some people returned home with an amount equal to the goods or food contributed. Certain high people leave with more than they brought. Commoners could contribute but leave with nothing. The contributions and the redistribution of goods fueled gossip for weeks.

My most treasured memory of those times is sitting in the feast houses beneath yams bigger than me. Pohnpeian yams (which are not the same botanical species as the western sweet potato) reach legendary proportions. Some as large as Jeeps have to be carried by twelve or fourteen men. A favorite variety reaches nine or ten feet in length and three feet in diameter. A single yam can easily be over a hundred pounds and many are estimated to be over two hundred pounds.

The rules of competition for yams are strict. At the section feast, each head of a farmstead may contribute food such as live pigs, kava plants, fresh breadfruit, fish, coconuts, taro, bananas, small yams, or purchased store goods. However, a man *must* give a large yam grown carefully from a single vine. Small yams are grown for eating; the large or unusual ones are grown for competition.

In all human cultures people work for a living or in some fashion seek what the Bible calls "our daily bread." They feed, clothe, and house themselves. They engage in trade, commerce, business, and economic activities. Beyond that, they will also use the fruits of their labor for prestige and status seeking. People can go to work by bike or in a bus or simple car. But some use Cadillacs, Mercedes, or limousines. The prestige factor has little to do with subsistence, survival, or just getting by. Instead, people of all cultures participate in activities that confer status and prestige and provide an outlet for competition. The feasting yams are in this category.

At a feast, the yam owner looks away modestly while his relatives bring in and display the huge yam. Someone says to him, "Your yam is number one." The owner protests, admires another's entry, and does not reveal his pride or pleasure. His modesty is as much on display as his yam. Exaggerated humility marks the behavior of Pohnpeian men on social occasions. This attitude stems from fear of ridicule or gossip. Boasting will only encourage others to produce yet a bigger yam in challenge. All believe that each man who modestly displays a prize yam has yet another, bigger one in reserve lest he be challenged.

This is why men surround their gardens in great secrecy. No one with good manners would comment on yams growing near the house, much less inquire about other places in the forest where a man might have planted another garden. Yams grow in segments; a single segment (several feet long) planted will grow into two or three more. If left in ground that has been dug up and softened, segments keep multiplying. Yams may be dug up, subdivided, or kept intact for presentation at a feast. Yams brought home from a feast may be replanted and expected to grow even larger for next year's feasts.

It is easy to collect names for at least one hundred varieties of yams, particular histories, and individual characteristics. As much prestige is earned for the introduction of a new type of yam as for a huge one. The little yams are eaten all the time; the competition yams are saved and given to show respect for one's superiors. The hard labor needed to produce these show yams is out of proportion to growing them for food. These yams are a form of conspicuous consumption that proves a man's industry, loyalty and generosity.

Some men achieve status in both the traditional and modern political systems. Being a lay preacher or an elected official are routes, though expensive and laborious, to success. The Protestant churches are staffed by Pohnpeians and the standards they set for them are strict. They usually drink no kava, but respect its use for others. They allow no foreign liquor, no dancing, no sorcery, no tattoos (a pagan custom), and no songs other than hymns. Visiting in Madolenihmw, we associated with Protestant households. So we drank no kava, but we attended church regularly. I was curious about the impact of Christianity and the mission movement (anthropologists often harbor negative opinions about missionaries who may destroy native cultures in their zeal to convert). I started listening to the sermons and prayers carefully while comparing them to the speeches given at feasts.

The Pohnpeians are enthusiastic Christians, and the gentleness and sensitivity of their sermons contrasted with the judgmental, often strident doctrines of the fundamentalism I had grown up with in rural United States. They love to tell Bible stories, especially the ones involving sex, incest, violence, political intrigues, or polygamy (the practice of having multiple wives or concubines). These stories were like the tales they told of their own past. The idea of the inerrancy or absolute truth of sacred Scripture held no sway. Jesus was as great a cultural hero as Lord Kelekel. The Ten Commandments and the Golden Rule were paraphrases of a moral code they expressed as cooperation and respect for their elders. The ethic of "render unto God what is God's and to Caesar what is Caesar's" was already the cornerstone of their political and religious system of homage to tradition and the Paramount Chiefs. They needed no personal conversion experience. They were born into this religion and grew up to its precepts as in the past they were born into a religion based on the reality of the spirit world.

One weekend, we attended the little chapel in the woods near Sohn Alpet's homestead and a feast in honor of the first birthday of his grandchild. I loved the serenity of his farmstead high on a hill. The raised wooden house blended perfectly with the magnificent tropical vegetation surrounding it on three sides. The fourth side afforded a view of the lagoon and the clouds that hung over the island. The inevitable feast house was small but filled with a special atmosphere. With my new status as a clan member, I was more comfortable than in any other household in which I had lived.

However, in the middle of a drizzly night, I awoke with the certain knowledge that I had to visit the little house. I had been assigned a sleeping post in the center of the family, a place of honor and security to be sure, but hardly conducive to movement. Emboldened with desperation, I tried to creep quietly out of the house. But I tripped over sleeping forms on the floor and bumped into the supporting posts. The pigs and dogs sleeping under the raised house awoke. As the dogs began to bark, the pigs decided it was morning and demanded to be fed. The animal cries beneath the house awakened the children. Adults awoke alert to surprise or danger.

I could not discreetly retreat. I could not even find my zories in the pile beside the door. The adults counted heads and commented loudly on who was absent, who was sleeping in the feast house, and who had the nerve to wake everybody up. I was grateful for the dawn. Roger had slept through the commotion. No one was angry, but several suggested candidly that I take lessons from young men on practical ways to sneak through strange houses in the middle of the night. After a cup of tea and a ship biscuit, Sohn Alpet appeared with a gun and gestured at me to follow him. At the edge of the clearing he shot a dog. "That dog barked last night for no good reason. That is why I shot him for the feast today. Now the other dogs will learn not to bark when they should not." He reassured me that neither he nor anyone else would shoot and eat a favorite dog. Perhaps this was a classic case of displacement. He could not be angry with me for nocturnal clumsiness, so he focused it on the barking of a dog.

We ate the dog at the feast. A ritual specialist who trussed it for the earth oven was fascinating to watch. I spent the day collecting information about handicraft techniques, particularly basket weaving. At feasts, people quickly and spontaneously weave containers and carrying equipment from the vast assortment of leaves and vines growing at their fingertips. They attribute little importance to these implements, which are discarded after each feast. But I consider them the most beautiful folk art produced on the island. The women of Sohn Alpet's family wove several intricate baskets for me. They take both the skill and the products for granted. They were, however, pleased that I sent them to my mother. All was forgiven.

The last major trip during this stage of the research was to the district of U, a seaside settlement called Nan U that was home of the Paramount Chief of U. Although I had enjoyed previous day trips to the area, I was dismayed to learn that Sohn Alpet had made arrangements for Roger and me to stay at the homestead of the High Chief of U. Although my command of the respect language had improved with tutelage, I remained uncomfortable. I had avoided even the suggestion of talking to the Paramount Chief of Madolenihmw and kept a strategic distance from him while living in Madolenihmw. Many Pohnpeians my age were justifiably anxious about exposing their linguistic skills before the nobility and wanted to avoid interaction with High Chiefs.

To make matters worse, I had collected dozens of examples of respect behavior and avoidance customs that were to be used in the presence of exalted persons. At one time, it was taboo to touch the Paramount Chief on pain of death. Although that extreme penalty no longer applied, the symbolic removal from direct contact with social inferiors was still in effect. Personal attendants do not look him directly in the face; they speak slowly and their intonation and vocabulary accentuate rank. Even today, the High Chiefs use intermediaries or ritual concealment to enhance their splendid isolation. Landing a boat or canoe or walking down the path near his house is accompanied by customs to show social distance.

Ancient legends explained the reasons for these customs and the penalties for violations. Although foreigners were slightly exempt from these customs, minimal rules for coming into daily contact with a high person were enforced. What if I unknowingly violated some taboo about dress, food, posture, speech, time, or space. How could I know all the proscriptions? Would my failures jeopardize the project? How could I remember all that irrational grammar?

I admit that my sense of equality had never been tested by public homage to those of higher rank. I had neither bowed nor symbolically prostrated myself to nobility. The Pohnpeians were bemused, even incredulous, that people in the United States greet the leader of the free world with a handshake and a "Good morning, Mr. President." Commoners, a status I was happy with, avoided contact with the High Chiefs.

Sohn Alpet coached us without the nervousness he displayed in Wene. He had requested that Paul Benjamin, a high-titled elder from U, work with us on the census and other data collection projects. The two of them kept busy, meeting continually on some political plots about title distribution that I found byzantine. I warned them repeatedly that they were not to engage in any plans for a title for Roger or me. Foreigners were occasionally given titles. The Peace Corps volunteers were inordinately proud of those they had acquired through the intervention of their adopted families.

Anthropologists, I explained, have to maintain some distance or neutrality in order to be objective. I feared that a title, of necessity from a particular municipality, would compromise our standing in another district and make the work of the project harder. As a U.S. citizen, I had no claim to Pohnpeian lineage and no intention of going native. Moreover, I knew that obligatory payments for a title were steep and that I had no category on the grant for such an honor.

Sohn Alpet and Paul Benjamin swore with solemn faces that they understood. To placate me, they collected long lists of title holders in all the municipalities and other technical information about the title system that I needed.

Living in the homestead confirmed my worst fears about protocol. The wife of the Paramount Chief was understandably jealous of his royal prerogatives and continually instructed me in speech and manners. In her presence, I sat silent like a good commoner. That inconvenience was, however, minor in comparison to the delight in the companionship and intelligence of Sangaro. The title of Sangaro is unique to the Nahnmwarki or Paramount Chief of U and refers only to him. I heard from some anthropologists and foreigners that he was a saint or genius, from others that he was Prince Machiavelli himself.

Respect observances from foreigners were of little importance to him. Although I was never alone with Sangaro (that would have been most improper), he sought opportunities to talk. Because of his friendship with Jack, he liked anthropologists and understood our need to record his culture. Mostly he wanted to pump me about the United States.

Sometimes he said, "Let's just talk; never mind respect language." He liked to speculate about U.S. technology. "Just look at the incredible machines you have. We see pictures of things we have no name for. I watched the airplane land at Deketik [landing strip], and I wonder how my ancestors could have built Nan Madol without cranes, bulldozers, ships, or the other machines we have now. Perhaps the Bible was right and 'there were giants in those days' who just picked up the stones and laid them in the lagoon."

"I have heard that you can open a garage door from a distance without touching it. What kind of amazing magic is this? Tell me how it works." I told him that you merely touched a button inside the car, but then I realized that I had no earthly idea of the connection between button and garage door. We agreed on magic as an explanation.

"Is it true," he asked, "that your countrymen have mistreated Indians, taken away their land, imprisoned them, and killed them?" I tried to explain but not defend the history of Indian-European relationships. "If you abolished slavery (as we too did much earlier) and proclaim that all men are equal, then why do you have those terrible racial riots and conflict between black and white?" I think he knew the answers to the questions he asked. But the question to which he was leading was crucial.

Finally he asked, "If Americans mistreat small groups of people whose skin is a different color from theirs, how can the Micronesians expect fair treatment at their hands? How can a set of tiny islands hope to negotiate our own political status with a nation of such power and prejudice?"

The negotiations about the status of the political future of Micronesia were on everybody's minds. What was the political future for Micronesia? Would the United States permit some kind of independent status for the people of these remote islands? Would powerful U.S. politicians put their need for military bases on the Asian rim before the rights of self-determination for small groups of islands? What would be best: independence, free association, statehood, a commonwealth, a dependency, or some other arrangement? How could the Micronesians balance their own ethnic rivalries and protect the interests of tiny atolls or remote islands? Could the people of Micronesia who had no experience of national unity cope with freedom, materialism, and international politics? I often heard the future of Micronesia discussed, but rarely had I discussed the topic with someone who had given such thought to the implications and underlying moral philosophy.

The trip was full of other surprises. On the third day, Sohn Alpet, Roswel, Paul Benjamin, and assorted wives and children arrived at the dock with twelve stalks of sugar cane and a big tin of ship biscuits. The sun was incredibly bright, and I felt silly, even removed, as I hiked up the hill with sugar cane stalks slung over my shoulder. Sohn Alpet insisted that we were participating in a traditional ceremony called an *aluhmwur,* meaning "to walk after." When high people such as Roger and I spend the night with a High Chief, the entourage and retainers of the visitors follow within a few days to present the host with sugar cane or kava plants. This is naturally followed by a feast with a pig killing, an earth oven and kava pounding.

I was dubious and entertained the suspicion that Sohn Alpet, who looked entirely too pleased, was making up traditions on the spot. Anthropologists certainly do not want people to invent customs, and I was alarmed by our sudden promotion to high people.

The arrival of our entourage with sugar cane stalks on shoulders interrupted a meeting of the Paramount Chief with some elected officials of U. But they accepted the interruption with grace. They pounded kava. Although Sangaro was a church leader like Sohn Alpet and did not drink, he served the beverage on all important occasions and expected it to be served in homage to him.

The first cups were passed, drunk, and acknowledged in what I knew were typical speeches for the occasion. I confess that I had been daydreaming when I heard my name called. I looked up to see Sohn Alpet sitting next to Sangaro, the Paramount Chief, looking very proud. My only thought was that my public manners on which he spent so much energy had at last pleased him.

Then I saw Roger kneeling in front of the Chief, who put a wreath on his head. "Your new title will be *Koarom en Dohlen Wehien U.*" I thought to myself, "Roger deserves a title." Then I realized just how cleverly Sohn Alpet had maneuvered us. I would automatically receive the female equivalent of Roger's title. Even as that thought crossed my mind, the Paramount Chief summoned me to his feet. I had been outflanked and had no recourse but to accept the title with as much dignity as he conferred it. My new title, Sangaro announced, would be *Karapei en Dohlen Wehien U.* Our titles translate loosely as "caretakers of a high peak in U." Which peak in this mountainous region, which is so steep that few live far from the shore, I did not know. I did know now that I was going to learn to love politics, place names, and high language.

Sohn Alpet, the rascal, regarded the title giving as a great coup. Refusing to entertain my now feeble protests, he began a series of lectures on our new status and the duties we had incurred. Our titles were classified as "konnoat," which is the royal word for "food." That meant we were entitled to a share of the chief's food of roast pig and yams at official district feasts. The connotation of this word is similar to that of gentry or minor aristocracy in English. In other words, we were no longer commoners with some obscure foreign status. And with Pohnpeian titles, we also had Pohnpeian responsibilities.

Pohnpeians who receive a title are expected to make a title repayment feast. Anticipating the elevation, some people save up for a long time. Our titles were worth a medium-sized pig and several hundreds of dollars in storebought goods (as our farmstead produced nothing but worthless cucumbers). However, Sohn Alpet had negotiated the payment plan, too. As he carefully explained, the Paramount Chief was a good Protestant and a lay leader in a church that needed a new roof. A contribution of money in lieu of a pig would be deeply appreciated. I appreciated not having to negotiate a pig purchase.

The next day, we made another procession to the Nahnmwarki's feast house with cash carefully wrapped in a leaf. I should have written down what kind of leaf we carried. Anthropologists are supposed to know details like that. But my mind was preoccupied with which category of our grant budget could absorb this peculiar expense. As we slowly entered the feast house for the title repayment feast, I decided on the public relations category. Government granting agencies accept the realities of field work as long as you use their bureaucratic language and explain nothing. Our faithful retainers brought gifts, and Sangaro was pleased with his new subjects who were learning customs so quickly.

At the feast of title repayment, I heard discussions about local history, title maneuvering, and more Lord Kelekel stories. I was beginning to like this character and to intuit some of the complexities of the legends. A good tale must be retold many times over and with each retelling new meanings emerge.

> Lord Kekelel became the first Paramount Chief of Madolenihmw.
> As was customary in those days, he had a number of wives. One day he spoke
> to one of them, the Great Eel Queen, who was on the verge of giving birth.
> 'If you have a girl, care for her. But if you give birth to a boy, kill him.'

When the child—a boy—was born, the baby bit off his own umbilical cord and ran away with the afterbirth. His mother was sorry that she had been ordered to kill him, and she cried. A man of her clan was bringing food as a tribute to the royal family. Seeing her tears, he inquired about the problem and offered to adopt the child.

The boy grew rapidly and went spear fishing every day. One day the ruler's canoe passed. The ruler [his father, the High Chief Lord Kelekel] called for the boy to bring him fish. The boy climbed into the canoe, breaking many of the rules of respect that Pohnpeians are supposed to use in the presence of a Paramount Chief. But the Chief invited the boy to the royal feast house in order to honor him for the gift of the fish. Again the youth broke the rules of etiquette by sitting with his back to the wall on the platform beside the Chief.

So Lord Kelekel made him Nahnken of Madolenihmw [number one in the B line, or second only to the Paramount Chief himself].

This part of the myth cycle has many versions and digressions about proper etiquette toward the Paramount Chiefs in canoes and feast houses (the very etiquette I have been afraid of violating). The story also explains why the Nahnkens (Chiefs of the secular or B line) have the privilege of indelicate behavior: they are regarded as the children of the Nahnmwarki, or the Paramount Chief. Later in the story, the son of the abandoned, impetuous youth raised to Nahnken by his father, himself fathers a son who becomes the first leader of U. That may be another reason why they wanted to recount this part of the legend. These myths may serve as a charter or explanation for certain customs,—such as adoption or bringing a token gift of fish to high people.

By virtue of our new titles, Roger and I would receive food tribute at the traditional feasts and sit closer to the front of the feasthouse. I was less nervous sitting under quarter-ton yams than I was by the smoke from the earth oven that often filled the front of feast houses. When I mentioned this at the title repayment feast, the men laughed. "That is the price of advancement. We say that smoke follows the high people. Now you are *soupeidi,* which means 'those who face down toward the earth oven and kava stones.' The smoke will find you."

While the gap between high people and commoners has closed considerably, the institution of chieftainship and the complex title system give a remarkable coherence and identity to modern Pohnpeians. While these customs have always been changing, they are in no danger of dying out. No one has an excuse for failing to serve the Chiefs and high-titled elders. After all, they say, the water in the bottom of the channel is always high enough to bring tribute to rank.

Nor would one want to anger the spirits that protect high people. One kind of sickness is caused by a lack of respect for family heads and high chiefs. The sickness will vanish when medicines and spells placate the offended spirit. If high chiefs are displeased, their followers and retainers must use elaborate means to mollify them. A special ceremony of public forgiveness called a *tohmw* may be necessary.

On the other hand, I heard frequent gripes about the high people. High people (it was claimed) do not redistribute their collections fairly. Gifts, flattery, and outright fawning over them are influential. Pohnpeians exhorted each other not to gossip about the actions of high people and then continued to complain in the time-honored ways their ancestors also probably used.

Later that month, I went back to Nan U to check some technical details on the census. I had notified Sangoro, the High Chief, of my visit and agreed to attend him at his feast house. The sun was hot and still, and I saw no signs of activity as the boat docked. One of his retainers emerged from a shady place to announce that the Paramount Chief awaited me and requested that I translate for a meeting he had scheduled with the new U.S. Navy Seabees contingent.

The High Chief was seated with his retinue and the officers of the military unit. I was once again struck by the perfect proportions of this feast house with its traditional lashings of coconut-fiber twine at the corners where the beams joined. One could almost believe that only this colorful and mildew-resistant sennit held the feasting place together as it and pegs had in olden times, but in truth, there were nails and screws in the beams.

First the polite formalities had to be observed. When the speeches had been said, the High Chief conferred a title on the ranking officers of the Seabees unit. I noted that their titles were lower than mine and that they were not expected to reciprocate in the traditional manner, as I had done.

At their request, I translated and explained the etiquette and expectations. The Seabees had been sent by the U.S. government to plan and engineer construction projects on the island. Their task was to find out what the Nahnmwarki wanted for his district and to build it. This was part of the recent U.S. strategy for building favor with the Micronesians in anticipation of the status negotiations. In actual fact, the Seabees were carefully selected to present the most favorable image of U.S. possible to balance negative views of its foreign policy and the Vietnam War. Tall, blue-eyed, blond, and incredibly innocent, the Seabees were breathless with the good fortune of being on a tropical island with willing young girls miles from the gruesome arena of the war in Southeast Asia. Gossip attributed many of the babies born to single women to these enthusiasms.

The main question was what the High Chief and the other political leaders wanted this smiling arm of the U.S. military to do for their district. The Navy men asked whether the High Chief wanted a boat dock, a school, a special road. I translated carefully. No, they already had all of these projects, courtesy of the hard work and dedication of the Seabees. I knew, however, that the High Chief wanted a new roof for the church in which he was a deacon. After all, I had made a private contribution to the chapel. He and I had discussed the strange, even perverse, view of the separation of church and state that is held dear in the United States. I explained that this principle was written down in our country's founding documents. He had heard the same excuses from other Americans. The Seabees would never be allowed to roof his chapel. But I wondered what kind of strategy he intended.

We drank soft drinks and ate donuts as the conversation continued desultorily. We mentioned the progress of the new road that would eventually reach Nan U, linking it with Kolonia. The High Chief occasionally interspersed the talk with a mention of how God had blessed the United States, what we Americans owed Him, and how much our technology had helped the people of the world. The Seabees gratefully agreed, thinking this a secure topic. I thought this was a clever approach to the roof question. The Seabees were accustomed to rapid responses and shorter meetings. For the Pohnpeians, custom and good manners dictated a slow formality with a subtle agenda.

The negotiations seemed at an impasse when the Paramount Chief announced firmly, "The Seabees can make only one contribution to the kingdom of U." Drawing himself up regally to a standing position, he elicited the attention of everyone in the feast house.

"It is the truth," he began, "that you Americans command the technology of the world. You have just placed a man on the moon, a feat lead by your great martyred leader, President Kennedy. Because of your skills, the people of the world no longer live in darkness." (He was referring to more than electricity, but I thought this was only another discussion of our wondrous technology as opposed to our dirty feet and bad manners. I wondered how to translate mild insults.)

But he continued, "All the world looks to you because of your power and cleverness, but there is much you could learn about making peace. We of Pohnpei used to war against each other, but we have stopped. You understand machines; we understand peace. In token of that, we [the royal pronoun] shall ask the Seabees for one thing only." At this point in the translation, the officers grew attentive. "We want a piece of the moon."

Consternation reigned in the feast house. The Seabees were ready to construct, if not leap, tall buildings. They did not understand. The High Chief waited and then explained patiently. "I humbly request only a small piece of rock from the moon. We have heard that you brought back many rocks from that journey. For countless centuries, all human beings have shared the same moon, all have pondered its presence in the heavens. Some have even worshipped it. But when you stood there, all of us saw the Earth for the first time. We share that Earth together, and the moon rocks are the symbol of one people on one sphere.

"I shall personally, at my own private expense, take this treasure to all the islands of Micronesia. They will trust my words. I will show them the evidence that the United States of America wishes peace, just as we do. Although we truly appreciate your nation for offering to build us another wharf, we wish instead to cooperate in bringing a better understanding between the people of Micronesia and America. The moon rocks will help people to understand that our differences in languages and in customs are small compared to our unity with each other on this planet."

At that moment, I understood why our ancestors bent their knees to kings. He was every inch a monarch. But for all his regal ways, he was negotiating with those of lower rank. The Seabees had glazed looks of surprise and confusion. After discussing with me what the Paramount Chief really wanted, the ranking officer agreed to relay the unusual request to his superiors. For the Seabees, the meeting had ended badly. They wanted to build and left frustrated. They had no intention of, much less official mechanism for, honoring his simple request. The High Chief, in his earnestness, had little idea of the sheer complexity of the U.S. government. I could not bring myself to tell him that the majority of our leaders do not even know the location of Micronesia.

During my visits to Nan U, I had learned much more from Sangaro than he probably learned from me. In his household, as in others I knew, keeping track of the children was tricky. The High Chief and his wife had been unable to have children of their own. Following the customs, they had adopted many, fostered still others, and asked others to live with them for varying periods. I lost track of how many and what type of relationship after counting and interviewing seventeen adoptees. Some of the couple's adopted children had children of their own living in the homestead. The couple obviously loved their children and, with Sangaro's high position, had much to offer them.

The habit of adoption is widespread in Pohnpei, as it is in much of Polynesia and Micronesia. I heard a great deal of discussion about it, and the censuses we did seemed to indicate that at least about one quarter of the islanders are adopted or adopters. The custom is called "lifting a child" or "being lifted." Ponhpeian lifting does not parallel our practices. No secrecy or stigmas are attached; everyone knows the facts. Adoptions are accomplished with ease, a concern for the child, and an apparent lack of pathology.

If a man or woman dies, siblings (particularly the man's brother or the woman's sister) will raise the minor children. This is a comfortable arrangement, since those relatives whom Westerners call aunts and uncles are already addressed in the Pohnpeian kinship terminology as "mother" and "father." Although everyone addresses several relatives as mother or father, they still know the true biological relationship. Because of the kinship terminology and the obligations implied, a type of secondary or backup parent and child relationship already exists. A spouse's child by a prior union, premarital liaison, or earlier marriage (what Westerners call a stepchild) is called a "discovered child." So the stage is set emotionally for adoptions.

In usual practice, a child may be given by its biological parents to another couple soon after weaning. The adopting couple will raise and provide for it as would be done for any natural child, including inheritance of land and status. In return, the child will care for the adopting parents in their old age, as would any birth child. Since Pohnpeians are deeply attached to their land, they must have heirs to honor that attachment through the generations.

The most common pattern of adoption within a family is where the biological parent is a younger brother or sister and thus owes some deference to the older sibling who wants a child. The importance of birth order in establishing seniority within the kin group and the blood ties between siblings are the strongest ties that bind Pohnpeian kin together. Junior members defer to senior members. Biological parents who agree to an adoption are showing respect to older relatives and insuring a better portion of land for their child. A childless older sibling may request a child for adoption from a younger brother or sister.

No special ceremonies or legalities mark the adoption, although under both the Japanese and American administrations, the agreement can be registered. The two sets of parents (or the single mother with her relatives) meet and discuss the arrangements, often with help of other kinspeople. A single mother who wishes to adopt out her child has full power to make the decision. She will receive compliments, assurances, and full support for a loving and dutiful act. The child grows up knowing the facts of parentage and will probably maintain strong ties with the biological family.

Adoption may be an alternative for young couples whose relationship is unstable or for young women who wish to retain their premarital freedom. In such cases, they can postpone parental responsibilities until maturity sets in. Others, who have embraced adulthood and desire children, will probably make better parents. Adoption may provide a gradual way to ease into marriage and adult responsibilities—in contrast to the U.S. custom where the birth of a child to a young couple, a premarital pregnancy, or an adolescent pregnancy has severe consequences for the education and employment of the parents, especially the mother, and for the health of the infant.

Pohnpeians value children extravagantly. Traditionally, birth control techniques were not needed. There is much sterility, however, caused by sexually transmitted diseases, particularly gonorrhea and syphilis, introduced first by the whalers and later by the militaries of several countries. Pohnpeians know methods of abortion, but believe that only a few unmarried girls would resort to such a stringent measure. After all, adoption of an infant would bring favor upon the biological mother, rather than censure.

I received tempting offers to adopt a child (other than a senior citizen and an outboard motor). I was a family member in a matrilineal clan and a member of the petty aristocracy. I knew of several couples in the States who had joyfully adopted babies. Looking for pathologies resulting from these practices among the Pohnpeians, I found advantages for all parties. Even handicapped babies found homes with experienced older mothers who loved caring for them. In other words, the emotional problems that may be associated in western minds with adoption are absent from this system. On an island that is 120 miles square and where every third or fourth person is an adopter or adoptee, a child is always close.

A letter from the field:

Dearest Ones,

Thank you so much for the lovely presents you sent. The sandals fit perfectly, but I must send them back before they mold terminally. I love the blouses, but I am amused by the manufacturer's instructions: "Machine wash and tumble dry." Not a word about taking them to the river, pounding them with a flat stick, and hanging them on a bush to dry. Although this method of washing is both fun and effective, it is hard on buttons and snaps.

My clothes situation is getting desperate. I have to be able to sit crosslegged for hours, get in and out of boats, and hike up hills without revealing too much leg or knee. I think I should dress appropriately (read, conservatively). Sears sells only "miracle fabric" dresses, which are no miracle out here. The synthetics are too hot, and Sears does not know that coconut milk causes permanent stains.

We had the canned ham for a party. But we are saving the bean dip until a ship brings some chips to go with it. The project people in North Carolina sent me granola. I mix it with powdered milk, and it tastes wonderful. I dream about food in 3-D Technicolor.

In Madolenihmw, we had wonderful meals, such things as fresh fish (raw, fried, and baked), mangrove crabs, yams cooked in coconut cream, fried and baked bananas, chicken soup, and pancakes. Last weekend, we went to another huge feast where we first had a lunch of rice and curry. I have discovered that it is better to eat first because, contrary to expectations, people do not eat much at the actual feast. Naturally, they had yams, breadfruit, three pigs, and two dogs. I have decided that dog tastes like roast beef. Sometimes it is tough, and sometimes it is tender, much like round steak. Personally, I think it is clever and economical to feed table scraps to dogs and then eat them. Sohn Alpet says that you should eat the ones that bark, not the ones who are personal pets. Before the arrival of pigs, dogs were the high-status protein food. Nowadays, pigs cost a lot, count as more of a serious contribution, and probably have a stronger ritual role. But dogs have, you should forgive the pun, a strong traditional flavor.

I have great pictures of little kids playing with pig entrails and generally getting bloody and dirty. They have such a good time following the adults around and trying to imitate them. They go off behind the feast house and make a tiny earth oven or carry around machetes taller than they are.

As honored guests with newly given and paid-for titles, we received some long yams that Sohn Alpet has taken to plant for us. Roger made a speech in Pohnpeian that he and Paul had written. I have decided not to worry about high language. I am learning as much as possible, but it goes against my philosophy of life to speak to high-titled people in the language used for God. I would be inclined to speak high language to show respect to almost everybody, but that is not the custom. The Peace Corps members feel that they have to speak it, but anthropologists don't believe that our job is to become someone else. Pohnpeians seem to understand that we are here to learn about their customs, not because we wish to imitate or join, but because the culture and customs are themselves important. Anyway, Roger found a good ground between high language and common language in his speech.

This season is winter in the tropics. The tradewinds are stronger and the rainstorms more dramatic. I think I would have to live here through more seasons to feel a real difference in temperature. It is still hot, hot, hot when the sun is shining. Because of the recent bad weather, the plane had to overfly the island. We didn't have any mail for two weeks. There is no mail delivery outside Kolonia, so on these frequent trips to other districts, we are isolated from the world.

I enjoy the company of all the Peace Corps volunteers stationed here. The number of volunteers relative to the population of the islands are, I have heard, higher in Micronesia than anywhere else in the world. That must be thanks to U.S. leverage and the U.S. control of Micronesia. I don't know, and they question the whole thing, too — how much good they do. But they are such committed, intelligent kids that the United States is simply better off when they go back home.

A bunch of us had a marvelous time snorkeling off a small island in the lagoon. This was my first close look at the extraordinary tropical fish and coral reefs of the Pacific. Coming back, we ran into the roughest waters we've seen inside the lagoon. Wave after wave came crashing on top of us. Very uncomfortable, but not dangerous. The winds are high in January and February. We were drenched from the rain and waves and stopped on one of those rare sandy beaches to build a fire to dry ourselves out. I was cold — a splendid, rare event. The remains of a former Japanese military installation are a fifteen-minute walk down the beach. I am fascinated by the remains of war so casually left.

All of us, Peace Corps and anthropologists, take the rules of etiquette at feasts seriously. You cannot dangle your legs over the side of the platform — ever. You must sit with your legs crossed underneath and facing the chief or highest-ranking person who sits on a raised platform above the main platform. You may not leave without asking permission — in the proper language, please. All walking or moving about is done by bending over and shuffling deferentially. This is to lower one's head symbolically. Pohnpeians take these rules very seriously.

Should anyone violate the canons of decorum, the Paramount Chief (the Nahnmwarki) may leave in a huff. In the middle of one of the many feasts we have attended lately, just before the food was to be distributed, the Paramount Chief suddenly bolted out the back door (which is actually the front door because it is his door). The food couldn't be distributed until the Chief returned. There were anxious looks and strained whispers. The second-in-command (the Nahnken) went to see if or how the High Chief was offended.

As it turned out, the Chief had only needed to visit the little house. Paramount Chiefs share something with commoners, although the word for it is different (naturally). Roger was secretly hoping that the Chief was angry, because there is a special ritual to placate him and seek his forgiveness. Roger wants desperately to see that ceremony performed. Another time.

Thanks for sending that picture book of dogs. What a funny gift. Everyone commented on the pictures of big, fat dogs. Very tasty.

Kasehlehlia,
Koarom and Karapei.

- 5 -

A Locked Box

For centuries our forefathers sailed throughout the Pacific Ocean without the luxuries as we know them, but they managed to give us a rich heritage, our customs, and islands we call our own. Destiny has chosen this generation of Micronesians to decide whether we want to lose our identity as a people and be absorbed into a foreign culture, or remain as proud and confident people among the community of nations.

—Speech by a delegate to the Congress of Micronesia

When the photographs of our trips were developed in the States and returned, I gave Sohn Alpet copies for himself. He examined them carefully and shook his head. Radiating disappointment, he said, "Look at you, this is not a proper way to act. In the future for pictures and in public, you must tuck your elbows in to your waist. Proper Pohnpeian women do not wave their arms about. You are permitted to smile a little bit, but not where your teeth are showing. You look entirely too——." He struggled for a word and the one he found could be translated as exuberant, animated, or undignified. "Everyone will know how you feel," he finished. "And that is not done in Pohnpei."

What he told me has less to do with manners and more to do with personality. The proper Pohnpeian personality is believed to be closed off to others. They describe their bodies as a vessel like a coconut frond basket that hides the contents. Seeing the basket, one can only surmise the contents. The human body has an exterior revealed in speech and behavior. But the inside feelings, the beliefs, the self is hidden from view.

Another favorite proverb says that "a man is an attic." A person's thoughts are hidden from view just as are the things stored on the shelf built below the house roof. Pohnpeians value concise, careful speech that observes the outward forms but conceals the inner person. Control over emotions in public is greatly emphasized. These belief systems also account for the elaborate development of formal etiquette.

People say, "Pohnpei is a locked box." This saying refers to traditional knowledge and its management, which is in the hands of specialists. Some legends are told for amusement—tales about encounters with supernatural beings, monsters, giants, or dwarfs, or romantic love stories and animal stories. But the tales that might be called history are rarely recounted in their entirety. The general content is common knowledge, but the details are known only to a few story specialists. These stories include clan origin myths, legends about local gods, the formation of geographical landmarks, magic, and medicine. Some can be revealed only on one's deathbed to a carefully chosen successor. This lore is not only secret, it is sacred.

The metaphor about the locked box is also about secrecy in traditions and feelings, as well as information anthropologists want. I am frequently asked whether people in other cultures withhold information, distort their lives, or lie. Pohnpeians are secretive. Many types of information are hidden. I wish I could say that I had a sound theoretical or epistomological basis to separate truth from lies. I have no doubt that I was lied to, manipulated, ignored, and tricked. All fieldworkers have these experiences. Sometimes we transform them into data and knowledge.

Had I gone to Pohnpei with the intention of investigating sorcery, I would have made little or no progress for months. My knowledge, actually a set of feelings and experiences, came unbidden. I have no thirst to know, much less to reveal, the identities or victories of the major sorcerers on the island. Much of the information I wanted to know, particularly the questionnaire about life-styles and blood pressure, was of no consequence to the Pohnpeians. They were relaxed about discussing diet, household composition, daily routines, and other nonsensitive topics. I doubt that they lied any more than Westerners do to the silly questions on surveys and censuses in their societies. I place a great deal of weight on repeatedly volunteered statements. The surface truth or nontruth of a statement is of less value than the underlying messages which are revealed by the pattern.

Incest is a good example. In addition to the heart disease project, we were engaged in both individual and joint research projects. Jack, Roger, and I decided to investigate incest, always a fascinating subject to anthropologists. But sexual activities are generally covert, and an anthropologist does not go about interviewing participants in acts of incest.

All human societies ban marriage or sexual relations between certain categories of relatives. That is the incest taboo. In the United States, we think of incest as child abuse and individual pathology. In traditional societies such as Pohnpei, incest strikes at the heart of social organization and is a crime against the blood relationships that bind people together. None of these facts, however, stops people from breaking the taboos of their respective societies.

Investigating incest was fun. I discovered that I had only to ask about Lord Kelekel. After the disrespectful son, Nalapenian, was rewarded by Lord Kelekel with the second highest title, the precocious youth began a series of amorous adventures with incestuous overtones.

> Immediately after his appointment as Nahnken by his true father, the youth went off to spear more fish. But on his way, his father's sister called out to him. And so he lay with her. This made him late to the walking cup of kava, which was being served in his honor. When the bearers brought the cup, his aunt performed the spell of the walking cup over him.
>
> They married and she bore him many sons. Nalapenian's son could not succeed him as Nahnken, just as Nalapenian could not succeed his father, Lord Kelekel, as Nahnmwarki or Paramount Chief. But the adventurer's son could become the Highest Chief. And so he did become Paramount Chief of another Pohnpeian state, which is now called U."

The story explains why the state of Madolenihmw has ceremonial precedence over the state of U. The royal lineage of U is descended from Madolenihmw, although the founding ruler may have been the product of an incestuous relationship between a nephew and his aunt. On this point the Pohnpeians are ambivalent. Perhaps they have fantasies about their own aunts or their mothers, since this is clearly an oedipal tale. In Pohnpeian kinship terms, the relatives Westerners call aunts are called by the word for "mother." The stories may illuminate the origin of customs, but on another level they reveal the thoughts within a society that are too dangerous or tabooed to voice aloud. The story proved an infallible way to ask about incest and generated many heated discussions.

The myths are full of stories and examples of incest. The most general category is called "evil gazing," which means heterosexual relations between clanmates, aunts, uncles, certain kinds of cousins, and inlaws. The taboo about having sex with a clanmate is not so strong that it is not regularly violated. The more besetting sin is to do it openly. Blood relatives are broadly defined, so the chances to break the taboo are correspondingly great. Everyone knows people who are guilty of evil gazing, though no one admits it of themselves. They have a saying, "If you follow the taboos, you die; if you do not follow the taboos, you die."

The rules of engagement for incest are like those for adultery. Couples who commit incest are generally consenting adults—brothers and sisters, parallel cousins, clanmates, aunts and uncles, in-laws, or grandparents and grandchildren. Perhaps they are alone together, and the attraction proves too strong to resist. Perhaps the attraction grows out of the taboo. Then the practical problem is where to go? Like adultery, the discussion centers on places, locations, opportunities. Stories about an adult coercing a child in sexual activity (the category of incest that dominates Americans' secrets) are extremely rare.

The most shocking violation of the incest taboo is translated as "eating a rotten corpse." This is sexual relations within the nuclear family. The most horrible form is sex between brother and sister and between parallel cousins (cousins connected to each other through siblings of the same gender, such as father's brother's children). Obviously, eating a rotten corpse is the metaphor for the most disgusting acts human beings can imagine. No one wished to admit this, and gossip provided fewer examples of violations.

"What is this about eating a rotten corpse?" I asked casually in relaxed settings. The response was immediate: "Where did you hear about that? Who is saying these things?" Then I would repeat what I had heard and ask for clarification. Some people were analytical; others told of specific incidents. All of the responses fell into the same patterns.

Incest is forbidden and shameful. People who do it are considered to be like animals. They can expect guilt, shame and punishment. One certain sign of guilt is dark circles under the eyes. Offenders will be visited by an affliction that is translated as "supernatural doom." The offender or close relatives will be punished by sterility, sickness, asthma, misfortune and eventually death. The belief that guilty people will be prey to bad luck and death is the safest and most absolute prediction in any culture. Short of such serious sanctions as dark circles under their eyes or death, rejection and ridicule remains the strongest social control against breaking the taboos.

Pohnpeians believe in supernatural doom but are vague about its source. In the past the clan gods and spirits caused it. Some remark that today the Christian deity has that power. Most have a feeling that customs themselves have enough supernatural power to inflict doom and bad fortune when they are broken. Supernatural doom is the penalty for sexual offenses as well as for breaking taboos about secrecy.

Roger's research project was in an area of maximum secrecy — traditional medicine, curing, and sickness. He was away interviewing for extended periods. During these times, Sohn Alpet and other friends (who always knew our schedules) brought assorted female relatives to stay with me. For a time, I did not understand what was happening. I craved privacy like a physical ache. After months of living in proximity to colleagues or in bustling households, I looked forward to an occasional rainy day of writing field notes, reading, or studying.

But privacy is a bad word in Pohnpeian. They expressed pity for my solitude. Don't throw me in that briar patch was my view. They respect privacy by pretending not to see or hear others in the same room. But no one should have an entire house to themselves. Furthermore, there was an element of chaperonage in the constant visits. Married women are expected to have high standards of morality and should not be left alone. After all, can we predict what will happen to a woman and a man who accidentally find themselves together? Proximity and opportunity are frequent explanations for evil gazing and adultery. Another interpretation of these visits was suggested by a colleague: protecting me from danger. While I was never afraid, someone had broken into the house and social controls for young men were breaking down.

At one of the many feasts in Madolenihmw, I sat next to an unusual woman. She was thinner and more publicly vivacious than are most Pohnpeian women, and we spent an enjoyable day talking. She reminded me of the assertive, funny women I counted as friends in the States. As a widow at least sixty years old, Iseh enjoyed a freedom of speech I seldom encountered among Pohnpeian women.

Several times I hiked up to her house in the hills above the end of the road and spent a relaxed day. Some of the Pohnpeian men I knew were overly protective, perhaps possessive about the growing friendship. They always questioned me closely about these trips. They seemed to accept Iseh herself as a good person, if perhaps not the best companion for me.

It was respectfully rumored that Iseh was a favorite of young unmarried men, who formed a line outside her homestead at night. A couple of the young men who had succumbed to her appeal said they were proud to be included in her circle of admirers. One young man gave voice to a common regard: "She is a great friend, experienced and loving. She refuses to remarry and cannot get pregnant. She's fun to talk with, and we enjoy her company."

Later, I tactfully asked Iseh about this (it is hard to know if one has been tactful in another language). She laughed, patted my knee, and gave me a cute lecture on the irrelevancies of age in making love Pohnpeian style. She claimed that age differentials were only an American hang-up and regaled me with stories of sexually active older women. "Besides," she added, "it's very good for my arthritis."

She, like other Pohnpeians, wanted to ask questions about strange western sex practices, such as homosexuality between men or remaining faithful to the same person all one's life. In return for my answers, she told me some eating rotten corpse stories and gossiped about the sex life of Peace Corps volunteers and the Seabees. She told me about a type of natural disease, a condition not caused by spirits, sorcery or supernatural power, called "bent penis." This was reputed to happen to men who engage in novel sexual positions with either inexperienced women or very experienced women from the Marshall Islands. Some women are alleged to be so skilled in intercourse that they can purposefully bend a man's penis, particularly if they dislike the man. The cure is oral massage by non-Pohnpeian masseurs.

The diagnosis is yet another opportunity for jokes, rumors, and teasing about sex. Pohnpeian men can usually name several other unfortunates whom they know for a fact have been victimized and deformed. Iseh said that men worry about it too much and that a bent penis is not a very serious condition. Some Pohnpeian men and some anthropologists take this as a genuine medical condition with serious symptoms and the need for special treatment. Others believe that it is great joke on gullible people. Sohn Alpet said we could not discuss such stories. Akina and Ioannes agreed that men like the cause, the symptoms, and the treatment.

Despite much previous research on Pohnpei, the lives of women were barely mentioned. I was only the second woman to do field work there. Jack's first wife, Ann Fischer, had lived there, but as the wife of a high-ranking official and mother of two babies, she did little fieldwork. The culture appears to be centered on men, and the most important topics of conversation are politics and economics. Men's lives set the tone of conversation, and women's lives are taken for granted. Women are not expected to speak in public, and what private power they may have is rarely discussed. For a time, I accepted both U.S. and Pohnpeian men's evaluation of women's lives.

Pohnpeian women are dismayed by the casual, open fashion western women and men associate with each other. Foreign women wear shorts, blue jeans, and skirts, which offend the dress codes by exposing legs and knees. Furthermore, they believe that western women are spoiled and useless: they do not perform the routine hard work expected of Pohnpeian women. Abiding by dress codes and exhibiting good public manners is one thing; planting and harvesting taro is reasonable women's work. But a sexual division of labor that includes catching rats with pride is going too far. I will always believe that trapping rats and disposing of their repulsive corpses is men's work—perhaps even a natural law.

My status was, seemingly, ambivalent. Childlessness created a barrier between me and the women whose lives centered on pregnancy, lactation, and the challenge of raising a family and managing a homestead. They were rewarded, I think, far more than my western peers for being wives and mothers. Being married, I was supposed to behave circumspectly and defer to men (and I did). On the other hand, I had the personal prestige of education, employment as a professor, and the government-sponsored research project. It did not matter that much of my status derived from the economic power of the research grant. In these ways, I enjoyed the status and independence of a man.

I had another problem common to female professionals. I was trying to handle two jobs, anthropologist and housewife. Being a domestic manager in a tin shack on a tropical island can be a full-time job. Sometimes I felt like a hunter and gatherer. I would go up the hill with an egg carton, hoping that the chickens were laying, then down the hill for a loaf of bread (my attempts at baking bread had been disasters). Next came visits to the little stores in an effort to piece together the rudiments of a basic diet. Fresh fish, fruits, vegetables, or meats could sometimes be found at other locations. Then the cooking, cleaning, washing, and the other myriad tasks of homemaking.

In addition, I did the laundry on the flat stone in the shower, but drying was a problem when it rained for several days. Pohnpeian women just shifted the laundry inside when it began to rain and outside again when it stopped, but I had no inclination to interrupt my interview and work schedule.

I had rigged nylon fish nets to carry my purchases on the motor bike, but I could buy only what was available and what balanced on the bike. That meant daily shopping. Of course, I met people and stopped to chat; soon an entire day had been consumed with domestic rounds. Cooking even simple meals of rice and canned mackerel or rice and corned beef (the staples of our diet) required much more effort than food preparation in the States. We also had company most of the time.

Some of the Pohnpeian men recognized my dilemma and introduced me to Klarines. I needed help, even in a shack, and someone to practice speaking the language with all the time. In her quiet, unassuming way, she became a friend. Unlike other Pohnpeians, she never questioned me, although she was sometimes mystified, even appalled by the foreign ways she witnessed. But she always kept her composure. On rare occasions she asked a favor.

One day, with other women we knew, she started talking about soap. The women were concerned that if Pohnpei voted for independence in the status elections, then U.S. money would cease to flow. They would need to know how to make necessities for themselves. U.S. soaps were good but expensive, and supplies were quickly exhausted. However, the traditional methods of washing seemed inadequate to them. Cleansing (clothes, babies, hair, floors, dishes) was very important in their domestic lives and so, they inquired, could I find a recipe for making soap.

I vaguely remembered my pioneer grandmother talking about how women on the Oklahoma frontier boiled wood ash and animal fat to produce soap. Certainly the island had plenty of wood and pig fat. After the third discussion about soap, I wrote my friends and relatives. "I know this sounds crazy, but I need a favor. Could you send me a recipe for making soap like our ancestors did? Check the *Whole Earth Catalog,* a hippie commune, Appalachian folk customs, or the local library."

When we had recipe and supplies in hand, Klarines labored many hours to produce a disproportionately small amount of lye soap which was strong enough to take the finish off cars. I had a new respect for the work of both pioneer and Pohnpeian women. These women had spent the same money for soap products that we in the United States do, but they earned so much less. I thought of all the kinds of soap we take for granted.

In return, the women gave me a recipe for ridding hair of head lice. This secret has stood me in good stead in New Orleans where head lice are endemic among all kids, including middle-class and upper-class ones (whether anyone admits it or not). I include this technique at the request of my friends who have found it entirely successful:

> Put a bottle of olive oil, coconut oil or other oil in hot water until it is warm. Apply the hot oil to the hair thoroughly. Wrap the head in a hot towel and do something else for an hour. Comb out carefully, strand by strand, with a fine-toothed comb. Leave oil on for several hours or several days, then wash out.

Bringing Klarines into the household was an excellent idea. The Pohnpeians would have been delighted if she had stayed with me night and day, but I balked at that, and we negotiated a compromise. She would chaperon me and work during regular office hours, and I would have both freedom and a friend.

One day, several men came by to talk to Roger about religion and curing. Klarines stood up and left quickly, averting her eyes. She refused to reenter the house.

One of the visitors was her classificatory "brother." The relationships between siblings are particularly intense, and sex between them is the worst kind of incest. Such relatives must observe very strict taboos and must not come into physical contact with each other. It is unwise for them to be in the same room because the relaxed sexual banter and teasing that marks some conversations is offensive in front of brother and sisters.

The terms "brother" and "sister" include what Westerners call cousins, and it is impossible to maintain strict distance for all of them. So a young boy is assigned a younger sister or a junior parallel cousin (one linked through siblings of the same sex, such as a mother's sister's child or a father's brother's child) with whom such contact is particularly tabooed. Klarines' behavior was entirely appropriate.

Where there is a great difference in age between siblings, more freedom is permitted. This custom runs deeply and may cause problems in schools where teachers are not aware of the kinship relationship of students. Ordinary play creates tension for children in a tabooed relationship.

Sohn Alpet had not been well through this period, although he continued to work steadily (he was paying on the motor for his boat). Roswel was unreliable when not under Sohn Alpet's direct supervision. Roswel's wife was expecting a baby, which was the alleged reason for his irresponsibility. He had done a good job on the census, but he did not have enough maturity or authority to help me write, translate, or administer the questionnaires.

With Sohn Alpet as a pivot, we had hired four more high-titled elders who represented each of the four districts included in the study. When we moved the interviewing and medical team into their districts, the interviewer-elders contacted the traditional, secular, and church leaders. Requests for cooperation from such men could not be refused. Among them, they had little English and even less social science training. But they had *manaman* (authority or presence). They were lay leaders in the Catholic and Protestant churches, spoke the high language for Paramount Chiefs and God, and between the five of them, knew virtually every person on the island.

One of the interviewers, Paul Benjamin, quickly assumed a leadership role, and his extraordinary tact and knowledge marked the rest of the project. In another world, Paul Benjamin would have been a college professor or a diplomat. He was literate in Pohnpeian, had been a schoolteacher and councilman during the Japanese administration, and had worked with earlier anthropologists. He possessed the gift, as a few in every society do, of standing outside his own culture and looking in. Although he valued and observed the customs, he was fascinated by how and why they worked. He was less concerned about conformity to etiquette than about our understanding of how the customs worked.

Developing rapport with this unusual group took time. They had never worked for a woman and needed assurance that their status would not suffer. The titles helped. Research was easier with a proper Pohnpeian title. Sohn Alpet had been right, and I was grateful for the doors he opened. I had more freedom, rather than less.

In their view, I was the number two chief of the project. Roger was the number one chief. According to Pohnpeian custom, the number two chief (the Nahnken, head of the B line) was the "talking chief." He (she, in my case) heard all the problems, frustrations, and special requests that could not be taken directly to the Paramount Chief. The number two chief has special claims to intimacy and confidentiality with which to present the problems of his subjects to the Paramount Chief.

But the division of labor that they had assigned to Roger and me was not the same one we used in our western-style marriage. For example, they expected me to work out the details of a transaction and negotiate with all the parties. Then Roger was to sign agreements and checks without being bothered by the details. I heard all the daily disgruntlements or the changes in plans. He felt left out of the decision making. Sometimes, he and I duplicated each other's work, reached opposing decisions on the same issue, or omitted an important problem.

I worked with the interviewers on the rationale and methodology of the project. Explaining social science in a language not designed for it was frustrating. Regardless of my explanations, however, the interviewers developed their own rationalizations about the research. Their primary consensus was that "this project is God's work." For them, any endeavor is worth supporting if it encouraged "cooperation," or "helps people." Elected and traditional leaders, farmers, and research personnel all do God's work. When I heard them praying about us in church, I was grateful to be writing the reports on the project. Try explaining to Washington bureaucrats or statisticians the religious connections in heart disease research.

My task as a fieldworker was to insure that the results of the questionnaire did not unconsciously project our western assumptions and values. To know more about blood pressure, we needed a questionnaire that would tap what people worried about and what they, themselves, saw as major problems and solutions in their lives. I had insisted that we ask them and not just invent a list of our own devising for them to pick from. Too many social scientists project their own fears, feelings, and definitions on others. Worse yet, since a questionnaire defines the categories or the problems, if the respondents have a different set of categories, the researcher will lose even the potential for knowledge.

The usual type of questionnaire limits the responses only to what the researcher considers important. For an ethnographer, variables, categories or issues are what the respondents or culture bearers say they are. As a result, some of our questions were less structured than in a standard questionnaire. My job was to make sense of their answers and to use culturally sensible categories for the final analysis.

As one example, we had to translate the idea of achievement motivation into Pohnpeian terms. Research in the United States shows a relationship between high blood pressure (and chronic heart disease) and key personality variables and reactions to stress. In the United States, we believe that some people are inspired to get ahead, achieve, succeed, excel or better themselves. The idea of achievement is often equated with individualism. To find success, a person may need to minimize family responsibilities in order to be mobile and self-sufficient.

To Pohnpeians, however, ambition is a respected, even ancient idea, and is not necessarily tied to job status and education. Ambitions are fulfilled by dedicated work for the Paramount Chiefs and by loyalties to section and district. Far from alienating an individual from his roots, this ambition strengthens family. In other words, an individual is ambitious through and for his family. An upwardly mobile man will have proof of success in higher titles, more prestige, and a larger share of the food distributed at feasts. To do this, he must mobilize his family to meet the persistent need for pigs, yams, kava, and the labor for staging feasts. Those with cash incomes will contribute money in place of agricultural products. A man advancing through the title ranks pulls his hard-working relatives with him, just as his older relatives lifted him up through the title ranks.

The traditional system fosters striving for success as much as any urban-industrial society, but it does so without sacrificing family loyalties and the strength of affiliation with others. The question was whether the Pohnpeians' mechanisms for balancing individualism and interdependency with others protected them from heart disease as the U.S. system did not.

We wrote the questionnaire to reflect what Pohnpeians told us about modernization and the stresses they felt in rapid social change. The pain of change was a staple of conversation. At first, these discussions were simple: I heard the same comments about places over and over. Other places are terrible. Those who defended life in Kolonia would complain about the rural areas. In the countryside, they said:

"The roads are bad."

"Those people do not observe the hospitality customs of old Pohnpei. They always want to be paid and to charge others, even their own relatives."

"They worry too much about other customs that are not as important, like respect language and etiquette at feasts."

"They drink too much kava."

"Too many family members drain resources; in Kolonia a person has less family responsibility."

"There is nothing to do when you get there."

"The weather is bad, too much heat and rain."

To people in the rural areas of Madolenihmw and Kitti, the metropolis of Kolonia was the epitome of urban evils:

"The roads are bad."

"The people there do not observe the *tiahken sapw,* the customs of the land. They make mistakes at feasts and cannot talk in public because they never learned respect language."

"They always want to be paid and to charge others, even their own relatives."

"There are too many ethnic types, outislanders and foreigners."

"Kolonia is exactly the same as America: cars, noise, crime, and big buildings too close together."

"The residents drink too much foreign kava (beer and alcohol)."

"The weather is bad, too much heat and rain."

These complaints about places were only a code for the deeper worries centered on the future of the islands and the quality of life for their children. Secrecy was never a problem in asking Pohnpeians about their anxieties. As they talked month after month, the larger patterns of their fears took form.

In the consensus of the islanders, the overriding problem was juvenile delinquency. This was both the specific issue and the symbolic category. Community leaders, including ministers, priests, the district administrator, and other prominent men had formed a Juvenile Delinquency Planning Council. They did not need statistical analyses. All sectors of the community, from the judges to the youthful offenders, agreed that crimes were on the increase. The chief offenses were stealing, drinking, breaking and entering, violating curfew, and brawling. They believed that these crimes were a dry rot that threatened their future.

In public meetings, they discussed the causes and the cures for juvenile delinquency. Just as people in the United States tend to do, the islanders blamed families, schools, and churches for failing to exert the proper influences.

Family life is bad for kids, the islanders said. Parents are afraid to punish their children and have lost control. Mothers are now going out to work leaving their children unsupervised. Children are too free to roam around at night. Parents do not take a genuine interest in their children's school work.

People also blamed community institutions for not being responsive. The courts are not giving enough stern sentences. Schools suspend students for not attending or for getting pregnant. Church youth groups deal only with ideals and not enough with reality. More policemen are needed to enforce the law. More vocational education, counseling, and placement services are needed.

American influences are subversive, they charged. Americans believe that individuality should not be suppressed, that children should be free. Schools should be allowed to beat the kids. They make no effort to teach morality and good behavior, as the Japanese did.

People blamed the negative influence of movies. (There was at that time no television on Pohnpei.) All agreed that not being trained for a job, not finding employment, or not wanting to be employed was a crucial factor in young men's lives. They feared that the rate of change, especially in the district center, was proceeding so rapidly that parents themselves could barely adjust, much less understand the pressures on their children. Everybody had a comment on what was wrong.

I interviewed a sample of policemen and prisoners. Since arriving on Pohnpei, we had been unwittingly involved in the "crime problem," which was connected to the "economic problem" and to the "education problem" and to the "breakdown of traditional authority in the family problem." Both prisoners and policemen were eager to speak their minds.

Policeman: "Teenage boys do most of the thefts. They enjoy it; they are proud of it. Their families make a big show of being unhappy about their children getting into trouble, but they don't really make an effort to keep their kids in line. Those who are influenced by western culture, movies, bars, and gambling have the most criminal activities. Drinking causes the assaults and trouble-making. The parents of children who get in trouble do not go to church regularly. There ought to be a stronger law putting responsibility on the parents for the children's crimes."

Prisoner: "I was thrown out of school at 16 for drinking. I liked school all right. I just like drinking more. I was thrown out so as not to be a bad influence on the other kids. I really would like to go back to school. My mother couldn't help with school because her husband was not my real father. I didn't have anything to do when I stayed with my mother but watch the kids. After the kids were old enough, I stayed with my mother's brother in U. Then I went to work on a copra contract and then another contract—plumbing. The government had some part-time jobs. I'd be happy to have a job again. I don't have any land. I do not enjoy the traditional customs. It costs a lot. You contribute pigs, yams, and kava. You get nothing in return. I have both municipal and section titles. My mother's oldest brother has a high title. I want to stay in Kolonia and get a job. I want to try and get my wife and kids back. [This prisoner had approximately ten jail sentences, from drinking (first offense) to grand larceny.]

Policeman: "One way to reduce crime is to give stiffer penalties—higher fines and longer imprisonment. People don't respect the laws. The police are very frustrated by the rights-of-the-accused rules. Maybe it is all right for Americans, but here a person brought in for questioning just clams up. Public defenders think they're helping the public, and they're helping crime. Corporal punishment [as under the Japanese administration] would not be effective now because people know their rights and wouldn't stand for it. Neither would returning the court's powers to the traditional leaders. Only the older people care about the traditions."

Prisoner: "I quit school after the seventh grade. I just got tired of it. I now realize that if I went back to school, I would not be running around and causing trouble. I never had a cash job. I was arrested on two counts. The first time, I stole a Scooter and fell down and wrecked it because I didn't know how to drive it. The second time, I stole from a bar. I got twenty months and a fine of $100, which my father had to pay. We committed these crimes because we enjoyed it. But I am ashamed, and I know that is a bad thing to do. I like the church sermons because there are good lessons in them, but I don't obey them. I run into a friend and we decide to steal or get drunk."

Policeman: "I have been a policeman for thirteen years. During that time, crime incidence in general has steadily increased. Most of the prisoners in jail now are teenagers arrested for theft. They usually steal money, clothing, and alcoholic beverages; only occasionally do they steal food. These are kids who have a lot of free time. The families of these children don't make them do chores around the house or tend crops. Corporal punishment would be the best thing for cutting the crime rate, and I say so from my own experience. During Japanese times, I was beaten and it really hurt. I was afraid to commit crimes, so I know it keeps people in line. I think the traditional leaders should have authority in the criminal process."

Prisoner: "I was arrested the first time because I was drunk in a bar and assaulted a man. The other guy started it, so I hit him with a bottle. Three months' sentence. After I served that term, I stole some liquor from the club. I served that term and got out and stole some more liquor from the club. I escaped from jail and went to my girl's house at night. I knew I was going to get caught. That added three years to my term. If I hadn't gotten into that first fight, I'd still have a good job. If I don't get a job when I get out, I guess I'll steal again. I have no use for Pohnpeian customs. I don't like kava; I hear people get sick from it. I like booze — beer and liquor. As I see it, the traditional leaders are dishonest. They care only about themselves and not about the people who do the work for them. Americans are O.K. I haven't seen any who are bad."

Policeman: "Giving authority back to the traditional leaders might work, but you have to change many things back to the way they were before. Think of what it would be like for people to start wearing grass skirts again tomorrow, just as people did a long time ago. Pohnpeians feel they are under the Americans and expect to be judged and punished by them or by people whose authority comes from the Americans. If traditional leaders were to do this, the hostilities that used to exist among clans and families would be recreated, since Pohnpeians no longer punish each another. America is fortunate in this respect because it's impersonal and people don't take out their resentments on the policemen and their families. More money and jobs might cut down on theft, but it will not help with the alcohol problem."

Prisoner: "I quit in the sixth grade because my teachers were cruel. Then I stayed with my family, and my father often beat me because I misbehaved. I don't know who was in the right, whether I was beaten unjustly or deserved it. I never had a cash job. I would like to go back to school when I get out. . . . The first time in jail, I was convicted of theft (seventeen dollars). I planned to buy clothes. The second time I was arrested for taking a dangerous weapon (only a table knife) into a bar and the third time was for stealing money from the Catholic mission ($500). I can't make copra, my family gave me no money, I had no job, so I stole."

Pohnpeian elders belong to a romantic and worldwide club chartered in the conviction that in the golden age of the past, before modern vices changed everything, adolescents towed the line and respected authority. The analyses of the policemen and the council reflect this belief, as do the statements of most parents of teenagers.

The elders believe that in traditional times, teenagers worked hard on the land and eventually received the rewards of industry, as they themselves had. They look back to a past when clan leaders, chiefs, and relatives punished serious offenses as a blot on the family name. Impersonal courts and judicial institutions did not exist. Elders laugh about the fun they had night-crawling. They remember youth as a time to sow some wild oats before settling down to adult responsibility. They are willing to overlook youthful pranks, practical jokes, and occasional wild behavior.

The truth is that the most useful and rewarding activity that young island males ever did was go to war and kill each other at the behest of their elders. Young men supplied the cannon fodder for the wars between the municipalities that the old men planned. But pacification in the twentieth century and less bloody forms of competition have made this role superfluous. The most common kind of murder, two young men in a drunken fight with machetes, is a contemporary substitute. There is little new about the brawling, curfew violations, rambunctiousness, and rebellions of adolescent males. Channeling their energy is a problem in every human society. Those who survive to a wiser, calmer maturity believe that the current generation of boys is the worst ever and will come to no good end.

Did the fault lie in the U.S. administration, which offered mirages of freedom and opportunity, seducing young people away from the old ways without offering meaningful replacements? Or was the cause in the power of the chiefs and elders who no longer had the authority to control the impulses of adolescence much less to order young men into battle. The delinquency council called for more counselors, more policemen, better schools, or better parent-teen communication, while acknowledging that such public exhortations have not worked in the United States either. Adults in authority, like the policemen, saw the (U.S. sponsored) administration of justice, with its jails, judges, a civil and a criminal code, public defenders, and prosecutors, as the problem. On the positive side, many young people do work hard on the land; others have succeeded in education, business, and government, while at the same time performing their family and title obligations.

Women, in particular, blamed the abuse of alcohol for juvenile delinquency and the instability of family life. They worried about feeding their families when husbands spent their income on drinking or about the embarrassment of sons "doing very bad things" while under the influence. They believed strongly that foreign kava (imported alcohols, such as the popular 151 proof rum) is historically and physically different from indigenous kava. One group of women even petitioned the district administrator to ban the importation of alcohol on the island.

The other truth about juvenile delinquency was that few worried about girls. It is true, they conceded ruefully, that girls are sassy to their elders. Girls want lots of attention and pretty things. They make babies. But girls did that in the past too.

At the same time, we heard stories about youthful suicides, which Pohnpeians insisted were increasing dramatically. I attended a funeral service for a young man in his late teens where these points were emphasized. The islanders associated the same complex causality with suicide as with juvenile delinquency: modernization, breakdowns in traditions and in family life, pernicious western influences, lack of community support systems, personal failings, and a decline of the work ethic. Yet their folktales and legends had many stories of young people who had hurled themselves from cliffs, sailed off in canoes never to return, hung themselves from coconut trees, or had otherwise taken their own lives in fits of unrequited love or thwarted ambition.

The concerns about crime reached a crescendo when a pair of brothers, drunk on a Saturday evening, attacked two policemen. One of the policemen died, the first such casualty in the island's history. People felt that a terrible turning point had been reached, beyond which there was no retreat. Apart from the symbolic dangers, there were older fears of clan retaliation between the families of the slain policeman and the young men.

Although officials in the Trust Territory's legal system took steps to punish the miscreants, the Pohnpeians did not trust foreign law to prevent local revenge. During this period of high anxiety, the Paramount Chiefs of several districts stepped in and evoked traditional customs of penance and forgiveness in a ceremony that they arranged for the families involved. The magical power of kava forced a reconciliation and averted terrible acts of revenge. American officials did not acknowledge the dangers of blood revenge or the power of kava and the Paramount Chiefs to bring peace.

During this time, I heard rumors at Stewo's restaurant about another anthropologist working in Micronesia and asking questions about the islanders' satisfaction with the current administration of the Trust Territory. According to the rumors, the CIA or the Department of Defense had sponsored the research in order to gain advantages over the Micronesians in the political status talks.

Anthropologists usually object to this kind of research because it is not published in professional journals or other available sources. Research that remains classified or secret also means that local people can be hurt. They do not know how to manage or manipulate the information they are giving. They may not be informed how that information is going to be used. If knowledge is power, then secret research, like sorcery, has the power to hurt.

Our research team took elaborate pains to explain our purposes, sources of funding, and standards of confidentiality, and to follow values appropriate to social science. We asked questions about people's feelings on modernization and the status talks and did not want to be confused with a project that some Pohnpeians claimed was a spy mission. With the Vietnam War at its peak, paranoia ran high, and anthropologists had publicly condemned colleagues for assisting in secret research. The gossip and paranoia about spies and spying paralleled the feelings Pohnpeians have about sorcerers and sorcery. We were afraid of the secret actions of others.

Furthermore, most Peace Corps volunteers, anthropologists, and other liberal foreigners tended to identify with the Micronesians. We were disillusioned with the shape of colonialism on the islands and with the potential for the destruction of native cultures at the powerful hands of U.S. business and military interests. Having learned the language and having lived with Micronesians, we saw their viewpoint. Anthropologists are conservative in the sense that we often champion the values of traditional societies over modernization and colonialization running amok. We have seen other indigenous cultures with their richness irrevocably destroyed. While the people may survive, the structure and traditions that give life meaning vanish. Already the potential for this loss could be seen on Pohnpei and in the rest of Micronesia.

The signs were everywhere, depending on your point of view. The elders were, as elders everywhere, dismayed by what they saw as the breakdown of traditional authority. Young people, educated in the U.S. system, did not want to learn the skills of farming and fishing, nor to participate in the traditional feasting and title system. They preferred foreign food, music, clothes, houses, and vices, or so the elders claimed.

The U.S. policy of pouring money into Micronesia (checkbook administration, as some called it) had resulted in failed development projects and a type of welfare state. There was a top-heavy bureaucracy with make-work jobs to which only younger males could aspire. Some Micronesians wanted independence and argued that they could control U.S. power. Others looked for some way to have material progress without selling out to an alien culture. Others just wanted material progress and the consumer goods.

Pohnpeians stopped me on the street to make points about juvenile delinquency or the status talks. Some believed that I had solutions. Quite the contrary. Raising the young and fitting healthy families into changing economic and political circumstances is a perplexing fact of modern life. Getting information and asking questions was easy. A locked box holds not only secrecy and privacy; it also contains the awful dilemma of raising children amidst forces people cannot control or understand.

Letters from the field:

Dear Parents, Siblings, and Friends,

Today has been the most unusual Easter that Martha and I ever celebrated, and I want to write it down while it is still fresh. Before the altar of the Catholic church in Kolonia, priests and Pohnpeian elders placed a kava stone. There, in full ritual splendor, they pounded and drank kava. The lifted communion cup was a coconut bowl. No wine or bread, only the sacramental juice of the pepper plant. The priests wore vestments, and the Pohnpeian men wore traditional loincloths and grass skirts. As the incense of frangipani blossoms filled the air, the celebrants anointed each other with coconut oil. A servitor sat crosslegged before each of the two priests.

What happened, as I have reconstructed the reasoning, was an extraordinary melding of rites of forgiveness and reconciliation from two ancient cultures. The church leaders had held long discussions to fit the theological meaning of Easter into a Pohnpeian world view.

Following the invocation and Scripture reading, members of the congregation came forward one by one to whisper their confessions into the priests' ears. That took about 15 to 20 seconds for each confessor. Then the kava was presented (this has roots in secular traditions, but I won't go into all the details). The first cup of kava went to the priest who prayed, "Our hope is not in this plant but in God's mercy and in the actions of Christ on our behalf. I will drink it in God's name as a sign of the pardon promised to all who believe in Christ." That was the Paramount Chief's cup. The servitor then offered the second cup of kava to the other priest and took the third ritual cup himself as a symbolic surrogate for the high-titled people present. Since four cups are ritually correct, the fourth cup went back to the senior priest, a substitute for the Paramount Chief (the Nahnmwarki).

The touchy part of this adaptation of the traditional apology ritual was the difference between the church's view of forgiveness and the Pohnpeian idea of the magical power of kava. When kava is presented in the feast house to ask pardon of the Paramount Chief, he must accept it whether the offer is sincere or not. Such is the power of kava. In church, however, the priests were at pains to say that only true penitence and inner faith will bring forgiveness. Kava alone does not improve matters or atone for sin.

In the Pohnpeian view, correct ritual procedures are more highly valued than evidence of good intentions and a promise to mend sinful ways. In the Christian view, God is less capricious or subject to manipulation than is the Paramount Chief. God is said to offer forgiveness only for true repentance and does not punish mistakes in the rituals.

I have been interviewing extensively about the rituals of forgiveness and the role they play in Pohnpeian society. You remember that I wrote you about the kava and forgiveness ceremony after the killing of the policeman, which ended a potential blood feud and brought public forgiveness. I could write twenty pages on these matters of theological interest, but I want to turn this letter over to Martha.

Dearest Ones,

Imagine, if you can, an Easter Sunday service that climaxed with stick dancing. Visualize several hundred people on bleachers in front of the church. The women are seated in the front, holding twenty-foot-long boards across their laps. The men are lined up in rows behind them. Each person holds two short sticks. As they sing, they cross the sticks against each other and against the boards to produce a complicated rhythm.

Women keep their elbows in at the waist, moving only their wrists and hands throughout the dance. The men's gestures are equally restrained. This is no "let's get rhythm and let it all hang out" occasion. They are dancing sitting down. I tape-recorded the entire performance, but I wish I could have made a movie of it. I have this gut feeling that many of the elusive meanings of their culture are revealed in those careful movements of hands and eyes.

Klarines and several friends have been at the house all week, working on their costumes for the service. I will send pictures, but for now, you will have to see in your mind's eye how they looked. Men and women wore bright red skirts, flower headdresses, zories, and coconut oil. Some of the women added black bras, white bras, or dark sunglasses. I loaned that dreadful red Maidenform bra to Iseh. She looked great. That's better than wearing it myself.

Do you remember long ago when that missionary family came to church and told us about living on an exotic tropical island? Then I was a frustrated teenager in a rural Oklahoma Protestant community who wanted to escape the restrictions of small-town life. You should have told me to be patient and that someday I would be a grown-up anthropologist attending a Catholic Pohnpeian Easter Mass on that island those missionaries talked about. The Hanlins are back here at the Protestant chapel and send their regards to all of you. Isn't life interesting?

Blessings and Peace.

- 6 -

The Ends of Canoes

Paddle left and paddle right, paddle mightily!
Our boat goes fast.
Watch out for roots on the crooked path.
And you there, listen
And the next one listen
And you, third man, listen
To what the first one says!

— Ancient canoe song

arly one morning, another distraught delegation from the hospital awakened us. Sohn Alpet, hospitalized several days for tests, had suddenly entered a crisis. The doctors believed that he would die unless evacuated to the more sophisticated medical facilities on Guam. Apart from the practical questions of whether the seaplane could land in the lagoon or whether his condition could be stabilized for the long trip, the family knew of no diagnosis, Pohnpeian or foreign, to explain his illness. They feared he would die in a strange land without the comfort of family beside him.

Some relatives were frightened by the possibility of sorcery; others were afraid to ignore its possibilities. Although the relatives were Christians, they were still influenced by old traditions. Sorcery was not to be discounted. The doctors offered no better explanations to assuage their anxieties. Some of his relatives believed that evacuation to Guam took him beyond sorcery's reach. Other relatives argued that removal put him outside the range of the curing ceremonies to lift the curses.

As the doctors at the simple hospital worked on Sohn Alpet, the family into which I had been adopted held frantic discussions. His condition, although critical,

111

stabilized. They decided to evacuate. We found transportation to take him and his family over the causeway to the airport. The seaplane from Guam finally landed safely. His tormented wife, daughters, and granddaughters, and haggard, silent sons and grandsons took their leave. We watched the seaplane bank over the Sokehs cliffs to race the setting sun to Guam. Late that night, I realized that I had just celebrated my thirtieth birthday.

The next day, family members waited at the hospital's radio for a call from Guam. Michael, the American doctor at the hospital, prepared us for Sohn Alpet's death. He had been comatose at departure and beyond the help of the island's medical resources.

The radio call, when it finally came, announced what I heard as good news. Within the hour of arrival on Guam, Sohn Alpet had miraculously rallied. His family, however, assumed the good news to be a confirmation of sorcery. His illness had no explanation; and he looked near death at departure. Why else would he have recovered so rapidly unless he had been freed from malevolent influences on the island? Here was the evidence of the curses they had fought against.

Senior family members quietly hired a curer to conduct the investigation and necessary ceremonies. The man they commissioned for the task was a lay leader in the Protestant church on Pohnpei. Officially, he claimed to have given up curing and sorcery-lifting rituals in favor of the Christian world view. Unofficially, his reputation for success in the traditional ways remained strong.

The day after the radio call from Guam, the curer found a curious stone beneath the sleeping mat of Sohn Alpet. This was a testimony to the fear that someone jealous, covetous, or afraid had put a hex upon him. Pending Sohn Alpet's return and an official diagnosis, the family started preparations for what they were calling a curing ceremony. They were pessimistic but desperate enough to try anything. Although I retained a naive trust in the effectiveness of western medicine and had counseled the medical evacuation to Guam, I was growing to accept their fears of sorcery.

Sohn Alpet returned after two weeks, alive but unable to walk. The hospital in Guam wired a diagnosis of lung cancer and gave him less than a year to live. Western medicine had given up on his illness. But the family was not ready to give up. Sometimes Pohnpeian medicines have been known to effect miraculous cures, particularly if the cause were also Pohnpeian. Following the impulse to which humans are so painfully prone, we decided to try anything.

The local curing system flourishes beside the U.S.-introduced hospital system. The fact that islanders will take sick relatives to the hospital first does not indicate their lack of faith in traditional systems. Quite the contrary. The hospital was free, a form of U.S. socialized medicine. Sick people could be immobilized in Kolonia while receiving the free benefits of western medicine. Meanwhile, an accurate diagnosis of illness was needed before treatment could be obtained. A disease diagnosed as a foreign disease does not need an expensive local curer. Some diseases are western in origin and therefore susceptible to cure by western techniques. But western doctors have little luck in treating "Pohnpeian sicknesses."

The indigenous curers usually make their hospital rounds at night. Once a diagnosis is made, they can often perform cures from a distance. One informant described the traditional curing system as follows:

> When a person becomes sick, an oracle [divination and omens] is sought to determine how the man became sick. Someone prepares the oracle from various leaves of plants. Then one could determine why the sickness was there. Perhaps a spirit had been angered. Then one kills dogs, large pigs, and brings much kava as an offering and prays to all the spirits. Then the sick person will either get better or die.

I was intrigued that one of Sohn Alpet's relatives, a sophisticated, U.S.-educated bureaucrat, supported the sorcery theory of Sohn Alpet's illness and had been instrumental in hiring the curer. As he explained, "Western medicine can diagnose cancer but knows no cure or no cause. How can you cure something if you don't know the cause? The Pohnpeians want to understand both the diagnosis and the cause. Sometimes with our treatment, people get well spontaneously. This is no longer an American disease; so we will try Pohnpeian methods."

The two curing cycles, which lasted four days each, cost as much as a major feast. Roger, in his professional manner, collected data on the plants, chants, techniques, and the theories behind the curing cycles. I had the task of organizing the financing for our contributions, arranging food, and sharing some of the emotional responsibility of illness in a family. On the last evening of the double cycles, we feasted and pounded kava. On the surface, the ceremony looked like any ordinary feast. No one made specific accusations of sorcery nor offered a guarantee of a cure. The speeches were, like those in my little feast house, carefully worded.

In participating in and observing the ceremonial round, I saw what the curing rites accomplished. The entire family had mobilized their concern and resources. Through the rituals they focused this power upon Sohn Alpet. They temporarily set aside the conflicts common to all human families. As witness to their beliefs, they collected money, kava, pigs, donated labor, and energy worthy of a major feast. In my opinion, this intensity and concentration had curative powers. At the very least, Sohn Alpet had the assurance of care and protection.

I saw, or think I saw, an interesting change in his attitudes after the curing cycle was completed. Returning from Guam, he had been pessimistic and depressed. He denied that the biopsy had shown malignancies. His moods fluctuated with flashes of uncharacteristic anger. When the curing cycle was completed, he recovered reserves of calm. He organized activities for teenagers at his local church and talked with friends, elders, and relatives all day.

I wanted to believe his assertions that he would recover his strength and be with us to complete the project. Although Sohn Alpet had trained his successors well,

I missed his sense of humor, reliability, and constant involvement in training me. All of us wished for a curing miracle.

Through the spring, the project had entered a new phase. The census was completed with the visits to Wene, Wapar, and Nan U. We hired and trained interviewers who helped to write, translate, and pretest the questionnaires. The threat of a dock strike on the west coast of the United States made us nervous since the bulk of the questionnaires had been shipped by sea mail. As we waited for the rest of our boxes from North Carolina, we also had to prepare for the arrival of the medical team and the final stage of the heart disease research project.

I spent months collecting lists of titles, clans, subclans, and the rankings assigned to them by Pohnpeians. We wanted accurate measures to determine a person's traditional status so we could compare this to his or her status in the so-called modern systems. For this, I had collected long lists of jobs, job descriptions, pay scales, and sources for household income.

Modern status is usually measured on questionnaires like ours by education and job level. In the United States, the status of jobs generally are classified into broad categories of administrative, professional, managerial, secretarial, skilled and unskilled labor. Pohnpeians, by contrast, classify jobs by analogy to traditional work and the degree to which the job is "advising" or "helping people." Thus, jobs producing or distributing food are accorded the same status as agricultural work, which is much higher in Pohnpei than in the United States. Cooks in schools are performing a community service equal to teachers or similar professionals. Appointed administrators or bureaucrats are not seen as "helping people," regardless of salary levels or status.

A typical answer to our questions about their work might be: "I work with the Catholic fathers in Madolenihmw, helping them and the students." Additional probing might elicit a description of the specific tasks performed in this job. "I give advice about boats and carry gasoline drums and take people places." Only independent inquiry and the accumulated knowledge of the panel of experts would determine whether this man was self-employed, a part-time boat driver, or a trained mechanic who owned a shop or fleet of boats.

Fortunately, all the interviewers became adroit at analyzing job descriptions and translating them into recognizable U.S. equivalents without losing the Pohnpeians' own sense of status and the worth of work. At the same time, respondents were reluctant to brag about themselves to others. A heavy value on modesty restrained them from revealing how much money they made or what status their jobs had.

We asked participants how many people were under his or her supervision. To people in the United States this means, "How many people consider you their boss and report directly to you?" But Pohnpeians have a larger sense of corporate responsibility. Teachers counted their students, credit union employees counted their investors, nurses counted their patients, traditional chiefs and their wives counted everybody in their district or section, and policemen counted all the prisoners in jail or on probation. Of course, everyone added their spouses, children, in-laws, and every relative younger than themselves.

We asked them about their source of income over a month's period. The answers ranged from the possibility of no monthly income to work on the land, salaries, wage labor or family contributions. But the statement "I have no money of my own" violates the value system. This seems to be the equivalent of a serious insult, "That person has no yams of his own." In fact, there are probably no people without money. People who have no cash income still have money because they can demand it from their working children, in-laws, siblings, or other relatives. Poor people on Pohnpei are those who are unable to mobilize the resources of an extended family in their own interest. One man with a wife and five children regularly gave more than a third of his income to his father and stepmother. Another man, having no salaried job, mobilized his two working nephews to buy him a new boat and outboard motor, each worth more than $500. The nephews complied, although they could not afford such luxuries for themselves.

These networks, affiliations, and the sense of connectedness made the Pohnpeians different from people in the United States who responded to the same questions. We thought this would protect them from the stress diseases so prevalent in the States.

It should be easy to find people on an island. But as we progressed through each stage, Roger and I kept losing the subjects of the research. The names in our code books did not match names on questionnaires. We had to locate our sample before the arrival of the medical team. Only when I sat down in desperation with Paul, Sohn Alpet, and his brother, Abner Olter, did I understand how our methods had gone wrong.

In common with many societies around the world, Pohnpeians change their names from time to time. They may have a baptismal name, a nickname, or a name to mark a new stage of maturation or to express some whim or personality change. In a matrilineal system, family identity is inherited from the mother's side, so there is no pressure on a women to adopt her husband's name at marriage. Through contact with the Spanish colonists first, then German, Japanese, and now American, the Pohnpeians have loosely borrowed the system of family names of the patrilineal principle (a man's wife and offspring take his family name). They understand and sporadically use this method of name assignment. The patrilineal naming system was, of course, encouraged by the Trust Territory government; many Westerners have difficulty in imagining another way of naming.

Having several sets of naming precedents available, the Pohnpeians may change all or part of their name or westernize their previously Japanese names. I found some women who were using their mother's name at marriage, adopted their husband's name, dropped it when they dropped him, and assumed their father's name. The children retained the last names of their mother's former husbands. A careful analysis of name-changing would probably show that these names are not just random or fanciful, but reveal cognitive aspects of social structure and

follow a complex set of rules. If this were not the case, many of our respondents
would have been lost. The interviewers always knew who had used a different
first or last name at some stage of the research project.

A lack of a uniform spelling system complicated the problem. The Pohnpeian
language was largely unwritten, apart from scripts and alphabets introduced by
the Spanish, German, Japanese, or Americans. The name "David" appeared
variously as Dapit, Dapid, Depit, and Tepid. Spelling variations made alphabetizing
impossible.

Furthermore, in traditional Pohnpeian contexts, an adult's name is not politely
used. One does not boldly ask, "What is your name?" Instead, one may circuitously
inquire, usually of someone else, as to another's title. Their title is the correct
form of address. But titles change and cannot be used in a survey. So our code
books listed participants by assorted names and titles; the interviewers could always
find them by intuition and inquiry.

Pohnpeians also take a fluid view of what Westerners call family or household,
and they move about the island at will. Seventy-five percent of our census
households included persons other than members of a nuclear family. Only two
individuals in the sample lived alone, and their situations were clearly temporary.
With extensive kinship ties and a housing shortage, an individual can live with
some part of his or her family in each district. Many Pohnpeians resided both
in Kolonia and on their lands in another area.

Married couples did not go on honeymoons and return to establish separate
residences. They typically resided with one set of parents when they were not
living with the other set. The composition of the family varied in each house from
season to season. For long periods, an individual or couple might live away from
the area they claimed as home while they attended school, funerals, cared for
sick relatives, or worked at temporary jobs. At no moment in time would all family
members (whoever they were) be residing at their true homestead (wherever that
was).

This movement between zones, the fluidity of family formation, and the
temporary compositions of households undermined our hypotheses that people
in different zones would have vastly different experiences with modernization and
corresponding differences in healthy hearts. We had used western assumptions
about life-styles and living arrangements. The Pohnpeians gently confounded our
ethnocentrism.

A letter from the field:

Dear Len, Joanna, our friends in Chapel Hill, and all supporters of high blood
pressure,

I should entitle this letter, "The Defeat of Social Science at the Hands of
Ingenuous Micronesians." I have had the hardest time persuading our
interviewers about the concept of sampling. The idea of arbitrarily using some
people and not others is perversity to them. Just when I thought I had convinced

them to interview only the people on the lists we spent months developing, I found a questionnaire of a Mortlockese and I asked Paul why he had included a non-Pohnpeian and a nonsample person. He looked at me with innocent brown eyes. "This man is like my brother. I live with him and he respects our work and wants to be included." Businesses here fail regularly for these "just like my family" reasons.

I think that the concept of a sample is the most serious gap in our respective world views. The Pohnpeians uniformly believe that the dual criteria of need and worthiness outweighs representativeness. In their mind, healthy people should not be given preference over sick ones. Young people should give way to their elders. Those who do not take church attendance or traditional Pohnpeian customs seriously should also be excluded. They refuse to believe in the notion of randomness.

Remember how hard we worked to promote the idea of blood pressure and heart disease as sicknesses that cannot always be seen? Now I lecture on sampling. But, sometimes as I talk, I wonder if they aren't right and we're wrong. Maybe there is no point to sampling procedures. I know, too, that your statistical experts back in Chapel Hill writhe in agony every time I use the word sample. Remind them that formulas and computer programs look very different when your feet have turned permanently auburn and you are washing clothes on a rock.

To solve the public relations problem created by these divergent outlooks, I have authorized complimentary interviews to deserving but nonsample Pohnpeians. The medical team will have do the same for the physicals. I have coded these in the code book so that they will not affect our sampling procedure. Rest assured that your computer will never see these.

Kasehlehlia.

A month after the curing ceremonies, I paid my last visit to Sohn Alpet. In his house by the stream where I had first visited his family, he lay on a woven mat. Surrounding him were fresh flowers and the evidence of constant loving attention. The women in the family moved quietly through the house, engaged in their graceful rituals of comfort. His daughter had prepared a soup of papayas (the fruit contains an soothing enzyme and is a favorite folk remedy). The simple house held no look or smell of sickness.

I had gone through unusual channels to find supplies of drugs to relieve pain, thinking to offer this last solace. But he smilingly refused, remarking that his relatives had some ancient palliatives for pain. The quality of care he was receiving moved me. At that time I knew nothing of the hospice movement, of organized and caring people who helped the terminally ill to die at home with dignity. Years later, I was surprised by the power of recognition when I visited another friend in hospice care. The women of Pohnpei, as women everywhere, must have been practicing this heartbreaking art for countless centuries. Care for the sick and dying was a part of their life that I had taken for granted, not realizing the commitment and knowledge they had.

As always, Sohn Alpet had something to tell me. "I am going to die and we must say good-bye."

My capacity for denial is immense, and no one had ever spoken to me like this. "Oh no, Nahnid, don't say that. We haven't tried everything to cure you. You won't die. You can't die." And so forth. I did not want to hear him talk about his death. I was comfortable with the practical problems, but not with the intensity of my feelings.

He persisted. "Karapei, be calm. How many times have I told you not to wave your arms around, raise your voice, and reveal your feelings? I have taught you respect, so you must listen once again. I have had a good, long life and die surrounded by my family. You will have to learn to say good-bye to those you love and to accept that death is part of life. Comforting those who are dying and grieving well for them is a gift of the spirit few are granted. This is the last thing I can teach you."

I cried, tried other avenues of defense, and finally relented to listen as I had on so many less painful occasions. Through the still afternoon, we talked about the arrival of the medical team, the trying trip to Wene, the beauty of Wapar, the great feasts, the little feasts, and other inconsequential topics. I told him of the financial arrangements I had made about the boat motor so his family would not inherit his debt. He was pleased and made provisions for its inheritance. He said that all of us who had worked on the project were like the ends of canoes that travel in single file with the bow of one canoe close to the stern of the one ahead. This is the meaning of work and fellowship.

We laughed and joked. We talked about death. He was right; I had much to learn. And then we said good-bye.

The next morning his family moved him carefully through the lagoon paths to his homestead on the high hill in Madolenihmw. His ninety-one-year-old mother, herself frail, was brought to the homestead. Moving one very old and one very sick person up the rocky paths was difficult. But a combination of litters, Jeeps, and many strong relatives accomplished the task. He was home and beyond the reach of modern medicine. If the curing ceremonies had accomplished only an acceptance of death and the loving care of a family, they were worth it.

In Kolonia, the work on the project peaked. The four interviewers, headed by the indomitable Paul, were working full time. Sohn Alpet's brother, Abner Olter, agreed to work with us and I was delighted to continue my connections to the family.

As usual, I faced the conflict between sound social science research and the determination of my island associates to mold the project in their own image. In my graduate training, I learned that the ideal sociological interview should be conducted privately with identically trained and objective interviewers. Technically, the respondent should not know the questions in advance and should not receive any help in forming answers. But this contrived style of interviewing was not working. Too many people were curious and eavesdropped whenever they could. Husbands were the worst offenders, although these intrusions were often encouraged by wives who asked them what opinions to hold. If an interviewer took his respondent to a private place, assuming such a place existed, they would be joined by children and inquisitive friends and relatives. How could isolation and privacy be desirable?

We also had the problem of distance. Some of people included in the sample lived in mountainous areas that were difficult to reach. In the inevitable wet weather, half a day might be spent walking to a house. Sometimes the interviewer would find no one at home. Moreover, Pohnpeian standards of courtesy demand a shared meal and attention to good manners. We were only completing one or two interviews per day.

Every place we went, the local people gave feasts for us—a tribute to the interviewer's high status. I viewed the ceremonies as time taken from our real work. But what I felt was immaterial. Custom is custom.

The solution seems obvious now, but until I gave up the stranger traditions of western science, I did not see it. The model was Sohn Alpet's work at the funeral in the hills above Wene. With the interviewers' eager help, we began a new strategy. As we started the interviews in each new neighborhood or section, one of the interviewers visited the local officials and planned a feast. We placed an announcement on the radio. On the selected day, all the respondents, community leaders, and people connected with the project gathered at the community feast house. We had kava, good public relations, a high participation rate, and a place to sleep.

The interviewers each occupied a corner, simultaneously interviewing the eligible participants. I checked the forms on the spot. If we needed further information, we did not have to spend half a day tracking someone down. Eavesdropping was reduced. We could discuss the project and answer questions, make appointments to visit households, and give the public speeches so valued by Pohnpeians.

However unorthodox for social science, this method fitted a dimly understood project squarely into the traditional channels of communication and group activity. The feast house method worked well, and the interviewers fell into the spirit more easily than the house-to-house interviewing in Kolonia. Residents of Kolonia tended to be suspicious about anyone who came asking questions. I had heard that some religious groups also went door-to-door, a practice alien to local sensitivities. I had to cheer on the interviewers when we worked in town. I did similar interviewing in a city once and hated it desperately, so I sympathized with their desire to be out in the country.

The pace of feasting picked up. Although the season of the traditional feasts had passed, the incidence of other types of feasts accelerated. On top of the feasts built into the research project, we attended several others each week. With the artificial infusion of money during the American administration, the number of feasts seemed to be increasing and the amount of money spent on imported goods had grown exponentially. While the traditional feasts centered on kava, yams, breadfruit, and pigs, these modern feasts featured the basins that typically contained mounds of cooked rice, taro, yams, boiled chicken, fish, donuts, bread, pies, and store-bought goods (cookies, Japanese rice crackers, tinned mackerel, corned beef, ship biscuits, canned soda, sugar water with food coloring, and soy sauce bottles filled with pig fat). On the top of these large tubs, suckers, Tootsie Pops, and gum were stuck up as decorations. At larger feasts, I saw brightly colored shirts topping the filled basin or even three-foot lengths of cloth wound around the branches and trunks of trees.

The amount of family income spent on this new form of prestige competition and the inherent danger to traditional customs worried the Pohnpeians. They did not approve even as they were drawn deeper into the expectations. They felt that the products of the land were devalued. Furthermore, the wage employment that fueled the redistribution was tied to jobs only poorly understood, the whims of the Washington bureaucracy, and a murky political future.

I wished for a computer to keep track of all the contributions: where the money came from and who received what in the redistribution. No one actually wrote down these facts, and the rules were in such flux that each feast, like a cocktail party in the States, was an innovation around a loose theme. Every feast was surrounded by gossip and anxieties.

Ironically, for all the food displayed at these huge feasts, people only nibbled. The basins were designed to impress and to be taken home later. The rice and taro at the bottom was feed to the dogs, chickens, and pigs. The children took the junk food.

I had long since learned how to sit cross-legged for hours on a hard floor and to accept graciously a half-cooked, dripping pig's head from my hosts. I learned to carry plastic bags or aluminum foil with me to feasts, and Klarines taught me how to cook the honored gift of a pig's head. It tasted delicious prepared with onions, honey, and soy sauce. The strangest feast food I ever received was an entire boiled rooster, plucked but otherwise complete with comb, eyes, feet, even toenails. It was too tough even for my dog. I probably did not receive back, when all the feasts were tallied, the equivalent of my contributions, but that is the way the system should work. I sent some very strange budget reports to Washington.

A constant theme of our letters was food. We were more than a year in the field and still having food fantasies. For the research project, which partially centered on changes in dietary habits, particularly salt, fats, and processed foods, I collected long lists of ship's cargoes of imported foods, sales at local stores, and daily diets of selected families in preparation for the nutritionist and her sample about dietary habits. The digestive tract weighed heavily on our minds.

All of the foreigners who lived like we did had periodic bouts of diarrhea, dysentery and parasitical infestations (undoubtedly related to poor sanitation and kava drinking). This, too, was a frequent topic of conversation, the details of which I have been urged not to record. Few of us bothered to have these diagnosed or treated at the hospital; instead, we engaged in a variety of folk cures. I swore by a three-day liquid fast of warm bouillon and warm Jello.

So chronic were these conditions among the Micronesians, they had developed a number of homegrown cures that I sampled and found very effective. I regretted that our research project had no money to fund studies about these problems. Babies were particularly vulnerable and had to be treated frequently for dehydration and gastroenteritis.

There was a sharp contrast between the healthy traditional diet and the seductive force of the expensive dietary habits based on heavily salted or processed American foods. One haunting example was the U.S. government's school lunch program. On a island of bounteous harvests, the school children were served white bread and rice, which they learned to prefer to breadfruit and yams. A generation of children was growing up to believe in expensive, imported food while the healthy, traditional foods rotted on the ground. We asked several very discerning questions in the interview about food preferences.

With the interviews and feasting schedule in full swing, I had to prepare for the arrival of the medical team. We had to house, feed, and otherwise take care of eight people for four months. I have to plan for housing, food, laundry, transportation, translating, and miscellaneous needs. Their schedule was very tight; to complete 1,300 physical exams they would need to work closely as a team for six days a week. I remembered the cultural and physical adjustments we made to the tropical atmosphere. The members of the medical team would arrive with the high standards of public health and comfort that I had lost by that time. Unscreened windows, outdoor toilets, baths in streams or rain barrels would not suit them. I dreaded to think what forms culture shock would take.

Kolonia was packed with people from the countryside and other islands in Micronesia. Housing was in short supply, and I could not expect a medical team to live scattered about in the local, makeshift housing. In the year since Ian's visit, I tried to find something large and suited to western tastes. Finally, I chose the attic of the Protestant church's congregational building. It was one large, unfinished room with a spectacular view over the lagoon and cool night breezes. I planned to partition off the room into cubicles, leaving space for a communal cooking and sitting area. Doors were to be made of sheets.

All of this assumed a supply of plywood, wire screen, and appropriate contractual agreements with the church. My letters to North Carolina during this period were filled with budgetary matters, shifting money from one category to another, and anticipating problems that could scuttle the project. I wrote to Ian to remind him to bring lots of sheets, and he wrote back asking about laundry facilities for the hospital coats. The arrangements were challenging. I wondered why I had bothered to learn anthropological theory in graduate school instead of plumbing and accounting.

The most serious problem was the toilet. Public health-minded professionals loathe outdoor wooden toilets. They believe in indoor plumbing that flushes. The

Protestants were proud of their almost new outhouse with a star on the front door and had no intention of paying to indulge the strange habits of foreigners. The solution was left to me, and since I had an almost religious fervor for water seal toilets, I built another one from the same set of plans. It was lovely; with its running water, it could double as a shower. I asked the workmen to install heavy handles on either side of the hole so squatting would be less strenuous. I also commissioned seats around the edges, inside and out of the toilet-shower room, to increase opportunities for socializing. Like the moss-covered stone church, it sat on the top of the hill. The medical team and the Pohnpeians alike were incredulous.

The previous summer, Ian had decided to import a special type of boat built for the rocky rivers of New Zealand. This jet boat ran just above the water on a cushion of air. With it, we would be free of the tyrannies of tides in bringing subjects into Kolonia for their physical examinations. The manufacturer had donated the boat (yet another alternative to the government's sensitivities about purchasing boats with grant money). The boat was cheaper than the alternative of taking the medical team and equipment into each of the zones we had sampled. Wene, of course, was too remote even for the jet boat, so we reluctantly planned to take the entire team there.

Everyone loved the boat, which even had padded seats and a roof. People not included in the sample redoubled their efforts to be tested so they could ride in the boat. Few research studies have a response rate which, without proper supervision, would have reached 125 percent. I suspected that a year's work of radio broadcasts, speeches, feasts, and careful explanations of our purposes was worth less in public relations than the appearance of that boat. On the streets of Kolonia and in every shop I entered, the curious and eager stopped me to talk about the boat.

Word of the jet boat's arrival spread rapidly through Kolonia and a crowd gathered at the hospital to see it. That same evening, a Friday payday, the radio announced that a twelve-foot-long crocodile had been captured in Kitti and would be arriving in Kolonia for display. Crocodiles are not native to Pohnpei. This one had probably floated in on a log from the Sepik River in northern New Guinea. For several months, the people in one of the swampy areas of Kitti had been complaining of lost pigs. Rumors of swamp monsters had circulated but were discounted as the fancies of people who live hours from the nearest bar. Finally, an enterprising group had baited a trap with a live dog and caught the crocodile, which had been brought to a field in front of the hospital. Most of us had never seen a such a beast, dead or alive, and thronged to the hospital.

That was a wonderful weekend in Kolonia. The bars were jammed after payday. People milled about in the streets, and teenagers raced borrowed motor bikes across the causeway to the airport. Everyone admired the boat and touched the crocodile. I collected some great "creature" tales about monsters, dwarfs, giants, or sea beings with strange powers. The arrival of the medical team was anticlimactic.

The anthropologists, interviewers, and medical team had to locate and question 1,300 people in the sample. At the hospital, we interviewed the participants again about life-style and personal habits. Then they were given a physical exam. That included a survey of a typical day's food consumption, smoking, drinking of kava and alcohol, and a health history. Every person had a fasting blood sugar test, a first-morning urinalysis, a chest x-ray, a lung function test, and a cardiology examination. We measured height, weight, skin-fold thickness, and other variables relating to high blood pressure. The examinations required at least one morning for each subject and two days for those who were part of the subsamples.

Answering personal questions, giving blood for obscure purposes, and publicly acknowledging the collection of urine are foreign to Pohnpeian notions of public health and modesty. Despite this, the response was over 98 percent, which is unusual in surveys of this kind. The success of a research project is judged by the rate of response, and we wanted to be like Ivory Soap—99 and 44/100th percent pure.

My job was trouble-shooter; I circulated through the community and listened. For months, I heard fears about blood collection and worried that the issue might influence people's willingness to participate. For years, medical doctors, physical anthropologists, and other researchers have collected blood samples in remote areas of the world. In this kind of research, a scientist does not have to learn the language or adjust to strange customs. But the Pohnpeians believe that a person's race can be detected in the blood. There is a similar folk superstition in the United States and I have frequently answered questions about "white blood" or "black blood." The islanders had lived under colonial rule for more than a century and feared that racial stereotypes buttressed by scientific evidence could be translated into government policy. This was a logical conclusion. Colonial governments are not free of racism, and the Pohnpeians were very aware of racial problems in the United States.

I explained again and again that race, which is only a cultural category at best, cannot be seen in blood, but some life-threatening diseases and health conditions can be detected. I knew I had been successful when I overheard some people explaining to each other that looking at blood is a form of divination or oracles and reveals important information for curing hidden diseases.

Some people worried that because the interviews asked about feelings and opinions, we could diagnose craziness. Mental illness is a cause for worry in all societies. But again I explained that the way people think and feel has an influence on their health, even if it is not immediately apparent. I heard a rumor at one of the grocery stores that we were collecting blood to aid U.S. war efforts in Vietnam. The Pohnpeians absolutely did not want their sons drafted to serve in the military and, indeed, did not wish to further that war in any fashion. I sent word through the interconnected channels of information that the syringes were too small for that purpose and that the foreigners on the project shared their opposition to the war.

Nothing prepared me for the trouble with the urine bottles. Every evening we sent the high-ranking interviewers out to visit those scheduled for a physical the next day. They were to deliver a written explanation (completely useless), to answer questions, and to give each participant a urine bottle with instructions to fill it early in the morning. Impressed with the authority of the project, some respondents asked high-ranking relatives to fill up their bottles. They claimed that such an exalted project would not want ordinary, humble urine. Or they asked healthier friends to contribute.

Although we had worked hard at public relations, there were other practical reasons for the success of this difficult phase of the project. The medical team arrived in the jet boat with several tons of equipment. Their charisma covered us like a umbrella. As time allowed, they participated in traditional feasts and ceremonies. They lived at the Protestant church and worked as equals with the hospital staff. The team gave physicals to people outside the official sample, including several Paramount Chiefs, many nobles, and their wives. One man, not in the sample, had a rare but treatable heart condition that had made him ill. He was a popular leader with a large family, and the response in his district was over 99 percent after he received treatment.

The demands of research were hard on the medical team. They had worked in areas of the Pacific where the physical conditions were easier. Research goals conflicted with their clinical instincts. They had been trained to leap in and save lives and were not schooled to the discipline of survey research. Equipment broke down and replacement parts were not available. The kerosene-fueled equipment was heavy and hard to maintain. They were dependent on the jet boat and the tides. I had hired two bilingual Pohnpeians to act as boatmen, aides, and interpreters in the clinic. But the burden of translating, organizing, and accompanying the medical team fell to Roger and me.

Letters from the field:

Dear Jack,

Martha and I wish you were here. We could put you to work. Thanks for the wonderful birthday gifts you sent us. An advance copy of the Sears catalog and a bottle of that new Clairol Herbal Shampoo was exactly what we needed. I suspect that Martha has gone "island-happy." I, of course, remain my usual calm and rational self. It must be a reflection of how long we've been here that these items seem so glamorous. Within hours, Peace Corps volunteers started to arrive. We all ate ICE and washed our hair with the exciting new shampoo. As we waited for our hair to dry, we avidly read the catalog and planned our purchases. I think that apart from letters, a catalog is the best link with home for us. Even though she has sworn off materialism and loves living free of so many "things", Martha even read the auto parts and home draperies sections.

I am glad to hear that your garden in New Orleans is growing so well. Mine has produced one ton of cucumbers and twelve ears of corn. Several of the corn ears were a whooping two inches long, and the whole crop didn't make even one meal. Martha claims that planting corn in the tropics is derangement, homesickness, and culture shock. She vows never to look at another cucumber. The bean and onion seeds you sent have made many snails and a few toads very happy. Lately, I have neglected my horticultural pursuits in preparation for the medical team, which will be arriving tomorrow — if the plane can land. I hope Martha finishes that dumb water seal toilet in time.

P.S. From me. I think I have solved the problem of how to find reading materials. I was desperate. I exhausted the meager resources of the high school library. I traded ice for books with the Peace Corps and have read everything the government sent them to brighten their exile. I even read Levi-Strauss again.

But now I have found a wonderful source of reading material to feed my addiction. On days when the plane is expected, I listen. When I hear it circling, I jump on the motor bike and rush out the causeway to the airport. There I throw myself on the mercy of deplaning passengers and the Continental flight crew. Shamelessly, I beg their discarded reading materials. Last week I got a Sunday New York Times! I have some paperbacks, too.

I miss libraries more than Mexican fast food. I have heard that Bronislaw Malinowski had a terrible case of book craving. If such a great anthropologist can do the things he did to find books, I can chase airplanes.

Dear Len,

I will give you a capsule review of the medical team. This is strictly my opinion, so don't file it with my official correspondence.

Ian never stops work. He is charismatic, generous, unselfish, and probably manic-depressive, although he manages it beautifully. For example, he paid for the transportation and maintenance of the jet boat out of his own pocket. But he is frightened of the boat, which frankly does not run well. It is a headache for him, but running or not, it has certainly helped the project.

The second-in-command is Dr. John, a real epidemiologist. He is an Australian, a staunch Baptist, and was a medical missionary to New Guinea for many years. He is an amateur but excellent anthropologist, so we have much in common. His gentleness and sense of humor make him a joy to be around.

Cara is the nurse-administrator. She runs the unit tirelessly and efficiently. I have never met anyone with such executive ability. She is the only reason why I have consented to do many days of incredibly boring data analysis. Nao, the nutritionist on loan from the University of Hawaii, and Rosemary, the other nurse, never gripe, and do their assignments of cooking, cleaning, carrying water, and other chores around the church and hospital. This is in addition to their professional tasks and the long hours of tedious data analysis.

Christopher, the medical intern from Michigan, is just plain beautiful. He is high on my list of special people who can be marooned on the same island as me. His gracious manners and competence have revolutionized the laboratory at the hospital — they adore him for good reason. I don't know how you found him, but you did good work.

Which brings us to Eric, who is a royal pain in the ass. I don't care if his father is someone important who pressured you all to send him over as photographer and handyman. He is homesick, but refuses to leave because he never finished anything in his life. He complains and is rude to the Pohnpeians — both capital crimes. I am perfectly peeved with him because he has never done anything to help as a handyman and strong back (which is what I understood he was sent over here for). Roger and I do basic carpentry, and Ian, John, Cara and Rosemary carry water. Last Sunday, they bribed Roger to take Eric off their hands for a day — that's how desperate they are. Now Roger is desperate to avoid Eric. I got stuck with babysitting him last week when we went to U. He disappeared, and we missed the return tide. I was furious, but he said artists can not be bothered with worldly arrangements. I know I was overruled about sending a photographer out here, but fortunately, he is too disorganized to commit the sins I had imagined. He just avoids all work. It is bad to have a weak team member when we are on a tight schedule and need all the cooperation we can get.

Of course, you know Pat, your anthropologist, who is the eighth member of the team. I am only sorry that he can stay for such a short time.

The medical team brought with them what looks like a lifetime supply of food. They have tinned butter, canned lamb tongues, and Marmite (a very salty yeast extract that they use like peanut butter). They have freeze-dried soups and vegetables. Needless to say, I eat with them occasionally. Ian knew from his visit last year how difficult it would be to gather food for eight people and still get the job done.

As a team, they are well-disciplined (but for Eric); they do communal cooking and follow the posted duty roster. I almost wish Floyd were here to see that. Ian won't let them take but one evening off per week to go to a restaurant. He makes them get up every morning to do calisthenics! Ian even organizes mandatory group activities on Sunday, their one day off. He still prefers to speak Maori, but all of them have learned a few Pohnpeian phrases, and that goes a long way.

Last week, they did a Caesarian section on my orange cat. I had loaned them Oang-Oang to catch the mice families in their dwelling. But she was probably malnourished as a baby because she is still so tiny and her pelvis is not right for normal delivery. They love being able to use their medical skills. In the absence of suitable equipment, they used bobby pins and Swiss Army knives. The two kittens are adorable and don't notice the large Band-Aid on their mother's tummy.

Just as I suspected. The Pohnpeians have given titles to the senior members of the medical team. At the feast given for them, I was privately assured that these titles are perfunctory, just to assist the medical team, and are not the equivalent of the honored titles held by Roger and your faithful correspondent. Innumerable people whom I interviewed about the title system formally deny such a practice, but informally affirm that many unfilled titles exist. Giving some out to foreigners who could not be expected to fulfill traditional obligations is a good use for these titles. In fact, it is widely believed that some of the titles are made up and are probably not even recorded anywhere.

The honor made the medical team so happy (and they deserve it). The Pohnpeians are uneasy every time they do this, however, because it leaves them open to charges of selling titles and exploiting their customs. Foreigners who receive titles usually understand reciprocity and make some kind of title repayment. As you can see on the budget sheets, the medical team paid their respects with two cases of soft drinks, a hundred pounds each of flour, sugar, and rice, and many yards of bright, imported cloth (I forget how much of the latter).

I spend major segments of my life these days in feast houses, where I eat canned mackerel and ship biscuits and sleep on a woven mat. My professional life centers around them just as Pohnpeian political and social life does. Why is this so much more fun than camping out in the States?

Thank you for your letters to Sohn Alpet. They mean a great deal. It is obvious that he has not long to live.

Kasehlehlia maing ko [which translates as "good-bye" in high language]

- 7 -

The Core of a Mangrove Log

Night after night, in the open hall of dance,
Shall thirty matted men, to the clapped hand,
Intone and bray and bark. Unfortunate!
Paper and pen alone shall honour mine.
—from "The House of Tembinoka,"
by Robert Lewis Stevenson

A radio call relayed the news we had been expecting. Sohn Alpet was dead and the family summoned to the funeral. We quickly gathered the funerary gifts, the sacks of food saved against the inevitable. Sohn Alpet had instructed me in the proper etiquette for these rites, and now I followed those instructions for him. We packed, contacted several family members still in Kolonia, and managed to catch the high tide to Wapar.

Although I had hiked into this area many times, the way seemed particularly precipitous that day. The sun was out, but an earlier rain had left the path muddy and slippery. The Pohnpeians with their graceful walk carried the heavy gifts for the ceremonies. With my usual clumsiness, I slipped and slid along the path, falling behind. My zories were caked with mud, and I had kicked pieces up to the waist of my dress. When we arrived at the homestead, I was barely presentable and had to be cleaned up by the women who greeted us. "I am not yet a women of Pohnpei," I said, hoping to diffuse comment.

The ceremonies would, as was the custom, continue for many days with little discernible beginning or end. The women of the extended family prepared the body for burial with obvious tenderness. Women who stand in a special kin relation to the deceased have the responsibilities of final care. The laying out was completed.

Sohn Alpet's body, covered with a hand-embroidered sheet, rested in a simple wooden box in the center of the room. Women and children came and went quietly near the body.

The men gathered in the feast house where kava pounding and gift presentations accompanied the earth oven and feast preparations. Roger had disappeared into the feast house, absorbed into the men's activities. Despite an intermittent rain, the muddy yard was filled with mourners greeting each other and performing the tasks of the funeral. We waited for Sohn Alpet's nephew, arriving on the plane from Guam.

Inside the house, I sat in the area reserved for family several feet from the body. The women and I talked quietly and hugged the grandchildren. Sitting cross-legged on the wooden floor, I felt the conflict between my professional self, who should be taking notes and asking questions, and my private self, who mourned the loss of a friend. Softly we sang the Protestant mission hymns with which most of us had been raised. "Rock of Ages" shattered my fragile composure. I cried quietly. At various times, close female relatives closed about the casket and wailed loudly. It is good form to feign grief, but such wailing is too intense a display to be maintained for long periods, and they eventually returned to their cooking. Ritualized, loud expressions of grief are appropriate behavior for women; men must display bravery and fortitude. For his youngest daughter, the grief was genuine. "Papa, don't leave us," she cried. "We'll take care of you forever. Now we are orphans." The women carried her outside.

The eulogy delivered by the one of the Protestant ministers was brief but frank. Nahnid Lapalap had been a man who fought for the right even if this offended some. He liked to lecture young people on proper behavior, but that was the custom of Pohnpei, after all. He was like the core of a mangrove log, the hard center that is left when the soft outer wood rots away. So have old men lost the ignorance and fickleness of youth as wisdom remains. A basket for money was placed at the foot of the casket because everyone knew how expensive this long period had been for the family.

In the evening when the earth oven had been opened and the kava served, the men buried the casket in the yard only a short distance from the main house. The grave site overlooked the slope of the hill leading past the mangrove forest into a distant glimpse of ocean. It was a simple burial. Men and women had separate tasks made familiar by repetition of family deaths. The children were present as usual, and observed everything, but they did not have to be admonished or scolded.

I remember the subtle exchange of feelings between the women. It seems strange to say that they took pleasure in my grief. They were flattered, perhaps relieved, that I knew how to participate in customs and in shared mourning. They knew the stories of the boat motor, the trips for the project, and Sohn Alpet's evacuation and terminal illness. Later in the evening, when we were again talking quietly, a relative acknowledged the friendships made within our families, "Now you are a woman of Pohnpei."

Klarines and I spent the night at the Catholic mission. Before the morning sounds or the palest glow of the sun, she shook my shoulder and, gesturing me to silence, led me outside. There we dressed. Although bewildered, I followed her swift movements as she led me down a narrow path for some distance to a boat landing that I had never seen. A red outrigger canoe awaited us. The single outrigger without sail had the traditional paddles and bailer. With Klarines doing most of the work, we paddled through the still black water of the mangrove swamp. When we reached the opening of the lagoon, the sun was visible. Still silent, we paddled along the shallow shores of the island of Temwen and into the ruins of Nan Madol.

This was a Nan Madol I had never known. The birds' screeching, an occasional fish jumping, and the sounds of the trees themselves lent immediacy to the thousand-year antiquity of this sacred place. Each watery path opened into several others, like a cobweb in stone. No paths intersected at right angles. Irregular plazas flooded with sunlight opened up at the ends of still dark waterways. It was as if, in stone and water, the early builders had duplicated the circuitous mountain paths and scattered homesteads of the main island. With the outrigger, the shallowness of the water and the tides were no barrier, and we traveled there as the original builders had intended. I came in awe and would have paid homage, had I known which spirits or gods to court.

On a schedule and with a purpose known only to her, Klarines began to fish. I could have questioned her about the techniques she was using, how had she learned them, what were the names of the fish she caught, what did women do that men did not and why. Instead, I helped. The secure and competent gestures that Pohnpeian women bring to daily tasks flowed from her hands to mine. Without talking, we shared the companionship of fishing.

My memories of that day are centered in the wooden seat of the canoe, the scream of sea birds, the touch of basaltic rock, and the smell of fish on my hands. When she deemed the fishing complete, we paddled slowly out of Nan Madol by routes I have never traced.

Directing my paddle strokes, Klarines steered solemnly as we headed up the other side of the island of Temwen. When we landed, she sorted the fish, strung coconut sennit through their gills, and made two strings. Taking the first length of fish, we marched along another path I did not know. Miraculously, I arrived with clean feet at a household that clearly was expecting us. Apparently, Klarines either knew or was related to everyone there. Someone fried the fish and prepared fresh fruit. During the meal, my host asked me about the nature of heaven and whether Pohnpeians and Americans will go to the same one. We also discussed whether people in heaven are divided by color and what other kinds of spirits live there. I asked him about the spirits he had seen or talked with. Then the meal and the visit were over.

How she arranged the canoe and the welcome of people I had not met nor ever saw again, I will never know. I do know that for one incandescent day, I lived as a Pohnpeian woman.

We returned in late afternoon to the subdued kava pounding in the feast house as the funeral observances continued. As was the custom, we laid the second string of fish across the new grave.

The next morning, I awoke late to the sounds of laughter. Stepping outside to retrieve my zories, I was drenched with a pail of water! The women in the yard were throwing water and mud over each other. Unrestrained, they made lewd comments about each other's body parts and sex life. I heard outrageously funny remarks about lovers and love-making techniques. I was wet and shocked. This was a funeral: where was piety and grief?

Throwing more mud on me, they explained that what was happening was custom. But everything is explained by custom on the island. Now I understand that what happened was a form of ritual release. An accepted moment of humor and fun broke up the seriousness of the presentations and ceremonies surrounding the death. Since then, too, I have been to funerals at which survivors tell bad jokes, laugh, or play pranks on each other when further seriousness cannot be sustained. The women nursed Sohn Alpet through the long illness, prepared the body for burial, and grieved for his loss. Now they gave themselves permission to play and to relieve their tensions. And I joined them.

Another, smaller feast was held later that same day. The Paramount Chief of Madolenihmw and many of the guests had left. The speeches on that occasion barely mentioned the deceased. The emphasis was on the glory of the section and the goals of mutual cooperation. How to account for my presence at the front of the platform caused a momentary dilemma. What was the best ritual introduction for a lone female, a foreigner? Would they just use my name, or would they say, "the American lady," "the Pohnpeian lady," "Mr. Roger's wife," the project director, or "the boss" (since several of my employees were there)? I listened to the debate and was pleased when they resolved it in favor of my Pohnpeian title alone.

Only later did I have clues about the men's work during these three days. I probably discounted their activities as secondary to the intensity of women's work. Roger's field notes of these events are completely different from mine. We simply did not attend the same event: this is the Rashomon effect in which two or more observers experience the same event as totally different.

From his notes, comments during the funeral days, and subsequent questioning, I pieced together the story of the tensions that marked the men's activities. To the uninitiated, this event looked like any of the other feasts, such as title repayments, marriages, or house dedications. Men brought the food and prepared the earth oven. They pounded and drank the kava. A master of ceremonies called out the titles of the high-ranking, coordinated the minute observances of proper etiquette, and placated the High Chief when standards were violated. The men worked very hard at feasts. They prepared most of the food and labored under a ritual burden that could sour in a moment if a high person were offended or if necessary steps were omitted.

At the funeral feast on the day of burial, the Paramount Chief of Madolenihmw had the seat of honor on the platform of the feast house. But in the middle of the ceremony, the master of ceremonies failed to call out the title of the Chief's son at the presentation of the kava. The High Chief, a proud and sensitive man quick to anger, noted the error. Someone immediately ran to uproot a small kava plant near the feast house. When the kava on the stones was squeezed out and the ritual four cups passed, the Nahnken knelt in front of the High Chief and laid the kava plant over his right leg. With a kitchen knife he cut off two pieces of the roots and handed them to the pounders. In a few humble sentences, he explained that a mistake had been made in error but not in meanness.

The Paramount Chief took a cup of kava and said, "I am very sorry indeed this has happened in the presence of people from other districts. They must see how the people of Madolenihmw observe the proper customs. It is not important that Nansauririn is my son, nor is the person of this man the important thing. But as title holder, he represents the people of Madolenihmw. In honoring this title, you honor our people and our district." In accepting the cup of kava, the High Chief forgave the error. Spared retaliation, the men in the feast house went back to work.

One of the lesser chiefs made a speech urging the workers to cooperate with each other, to work slowly, and to make no mistakes. Another chief asked the workers not to be distracted by the discomfort caused by the rain and cold. "Do not think of the difficulties but of the heavy responsibilities of this day. Think only of the love we bear this man who has died."

Apparently the Paramount Chief was already irritated by confusion and noise from the preparation of the earth oven. The ritual error was the last straw. But his son, over whom this furor had broken, counseled his father, "Try to educate the people in our customs. Don't just fly off the handle as did the Paramount Chiefs of the past." He resorted to the saying, "Chiefs are like hibiscus in the wind." They must be flexible and bend. Perhaps the son, Nansauririn, had been at fault by not first paying homage to his father, the High Chief. But as a Protestant minister, he had a conflicting role in comforting the bereaved inside the house. In a classic case of displacement, the father took the chiefly privilege of directing his anger toward someone else of lower rank.

My notes show that the Paramount Chief's displeasure was also assuaged by an offering collected for his new district feast house.

Another tension simmered beneath the surface. About a week before his death, Sohn Alpet requested the Paramount Chief of Madolenihmw to pass on the title of Nahnid Lapalap to one of his sons. The high title had been rewarded to Sohn Alpet as a returning warrior from World War II in New Guinea. Ordinarily, such a high title awarded under special circumstances would not stay in the family. This high title should have gone to another clan and under the matrilineal principle would not have been passed from father to son. People generally agreed that the title did not belong in Sohn Alpet's family and expected the Nahnmwarki to take it away in accordance with tradition. A death bed request, however, merited attention. Speculation about the decision of the High Chief ran high.

But the High Chief decreed a suspension of work on the new municipal feast house in honor of Sohn Alpet's last days and the funeral week. Out of respect, the announcement of the new title holder was withheld until all of the reciprocal exchanges and kava drinking had ended. When the funeral observances were over, the announcement of a new Nahnid Lapalap, not Sohn Alpet's son, was made.

Roger had returned to Kolonia after the funeral, and his field notes once again reflect a different experience from mine:

> After the burial, which took place at sunset, I returned to Kolonia, traveling on the lagoon for more than two hours after dark. All we had to keep us off the reef was the experience of the boatman and a measly flashlight. This, believe me, was downright scary. Of course, the Pohnpeians frequently drive their boats on the lagoon after dark and don't think much about it. But I don't care to do it again, if I can avoid it.

For me, the trip home on the lagoon several evenings later was peaceful and calm. I grieved for a lost friend, but I had prepared for the death, and the mourning observances had reconciled me to the fact. The moon shining on the water was lovely and I felt at ease with my adopted family. In retrospect, I think that the trip came as close to a mountain top experience as I am ever likely to have. That night, on the lagoon, I decided to have a baby. And the next day, I got pregnant.

Meanwhile, the work of the medical team was moving ahead rapidly. The last four weeks of the research project were to be spent in Wene. We had to arrange for a barge to carry the kerosene refrigerators, barrels, boxes, and the laboratory and medical supplies. This involved the assistance of U.S. military representatives and Trust Territory officials. Timing was crucial. The barge had to be loaded after all the medical examinations were finished in the Kolonia hospital. But sailing had to coincide with the month's highest tide on the other side of the island, so the laden barge could get through the mangrove swamp and to the landing dock of Wene.

Roger and I tossed a coin for the honor of returning to Wene, and I lost. He stayed in Kolonia to coordinate the problems and activities of the medical team. Through the concerted efforts of the medical team and the anthropological team, we had found a way to lose Eric, the pain. Unfortunately, we also lost Christopher, the medical resident, who returned to the States. Our team was becoming compact.

I asked Sohn Alpet's brother, Abner Olter (whose title was Kaniki Ririn), to represent the interviewers. His wit and intelligence kept me sane while we went to considerable trouble to find chaperons so we would not be the target of gossip. My lodging was in the impressive homestead of Oaron Kiti, whose feast house dedication we had attended the year before. His family placed me in one of the cool rooms. Close by the path leading to the dock were two lovely rock-rimmed streams that formed bathing pools.

My arrangements included teams of men to unload the barge and water buffalo to carry everything up the hill to the dispensary, and housing for the medical team at the homestead of Dr. Franko, where we stayed our first time in Wene. They had to have a shower and a little house that met some reasonable standards of public health. The house had two large bedrooms, a kitchen, and a long, enclosed veranda.

I dreaded the arrival of the medical team and the accelerated pace. Food was a headache. Typical of my experience in Wene, a number of large scale funerals had stripped the community of most ordinary foodstuffs. They had not yet recouped their energy or supplies. As a result of a continuing dock strike on the west coast of the United States, several months had passed without the arrival of a supply ship. Wene was completely sold out of products from the States. A few Japanese and Australian goods had trickled into the area. Although the medical team had their ubiquitous tinned lamb tongues, Marmite, and corned beef, they needed fresh bread and fresh produce.

For the bread, I had to find a reliable source of flour, as well as a reliable baker. Contracts had to be let for each item as well the related services, such as delivery. Negotiations over money were a constant headache.

On one level, I sympathized with the people of Wene. They lived in a beautiful but remote area where the opportunities for cash income, much less economic development, were extremely limited. The decision of the Peace Corps to locate its first training center in this isolated community only whetted the expectations of local people. Now they saw all foreigners, especially Americans, as groups who should be willing to drop bundles of cash on their doorsteps. The payments they expected for various jobs bore no relationship to U.S. pay scales. The generosity and spirit of cooperation that Pohnpeians might choose to show to individual visitors could not be extended to large groups. They needed the money and they believed we had it.

The situation was further complicated by the kind of factions that exist in all small communities. I called the two factions in Wene, the highlanders and the lowlanders. The latter group lived in the area near the dock, the Catholic mission, and the little store. The leaders of the other group had homesteads spaced far back into the mountains. I could not hire an individual for a job without consulting the leaders who manipulated the labor supply and acted as subcontractors. Most discussions I had with them were subtle harangues against the opposition. "Those people down there [or up there] will not work well. Your things will get lost or stolen. You must trust us instead. Now let us see how much our cooperation will cost."

Our liaison with the Kolonia hospital was the omnipresent Dr. Franko. He was also in charge of the tiny dispensary where we intended to work. His relatives were in both factions, and his house was the only suitable dwelling in the community for the team. He wanted to be treated as a western medical entrepreneur for half the day and as a high-titled Pohnpeian elder the other half. I heard tiny hints of blackmail.

For an anthropologist, rivalries between warring factions are bread and butter. Through such tensions, we can learn how the society, the value systems, power, and leadership are structured. Usually, anthropologists are able to observe, describe, and explain. There is a certain detachment, even pleasure, in the knowledge of cultural functions. But I was working under the pressure of the medical team's schedule, its needs, and the Pohnpeian certainty that I had unlimited funds to spend. I could not be a dispassionate observer.

The arrival of the medical team with tons of goods was perfectly timed with the tides. All went well as the lowland faction unloaded the barge. But late that night Cora, one of the nurses, came down the path with an urgent problem. A large family had moved into the kitchen of their rented house. With only four rooms, the house was already crowded. I tramped back up the hill with misgivings. I had spent months negotiating what I thought was a watertight contract with Dr. Franko for this housing. But as he innocently explained, "You didn't say that no one was supposed to occupy the kitchen. In our customs, families like to stay near each other."

He had other manipulative strategies. I think that he had deliberately moved in part of his extended family in hopes of filling jobs for the medical team and having access to more money. But the medical team, none of whom spoke Pohnpeian, did their own housework and had no intention of sharing living quarters (a feeling with which I totally sympathized). The repercussions of this difficult transaction continued to surface in indirect ways.

My own situation was stressful because of my pregnancy. I admired the family with which I was staying and delighted in the atmosphere of this little tropical world. But I was ravenous for foods I could not have. Some days the nausea of pregnancy came in heavy waves. I wanted milk, temperate-zone fruits, and coffee from the Cafe du Monde in New Orleans. No one in the community was going to starve, including me, but the food arrived in strange patterns. I remember eating ship biscuits and mangrove crabs for several days. I spent a lot of time hunting for papayas, which are known for settling the stomach, but none of the trees were producing.

Residents staged several feasts during my first weeks of pregnancy, and cooked dog was abundant. The tiny commissary carried only Japanese rice crackers. So during periods when the nausea abated, I ate roast dog and rice crackers. To this day, I cannot stand the thought of eating a Japanese rice cracker.

One day the most amazing thing happened. Nao, the nutritionist on the project, was visited by her husband, a well-known photographer from Hawaii who had brought a crate of vegetables for us. Incredible, edible vegetables: broccoli, large red tomatoes, Romaine lettuce, and other such delicacies. The medical team with its health-food leanings and I with my incessant food fantasies fell ravenously upon the vegetables, eating them raw. We cooked them and gorged a second time. But our intestinal tracts, deprived for too long, revolted, and the next day a green, distracted team had trouble working. My case was worse, since the nurses and doctors had given me the lion's share in honor of my condition and longer period of deprivation. Whatever price I paid for this indulgence, I will never forget that first bite of raw broccoli.

Every evening I drank kava, either at my host's house or at neighboring homesteads. Kava gatherings are occasions for patching up differences and forgetting grievances. Kava has a special power to bring about good feelings, and I needed that. During this period, I made many speeches with a kava cup in my hand, explaining over again the purposes and activities of the project. Drinking kava is said to be good for pregnant women. It insures that the child will have healthy, clear skin.

On another evening, I accepted a cup of kava from a gracious young man who said he had heard of our work at the hospital. "I have respect for the work of the hospital because I am an outpatient there. In the leprosy clinic." I gulped and added leprosy to the list of twelve dreaded diseases that one might get from drinking kava.

That evening I had watched the men add water from the nearby stream to the hibiscus bark used to squeeze the kava roots. At the same time, I saw the pigs peeing and people splashing in the stream. God will have to protect anthropologists and other strange people who have suspended their faith in the germ theory of disease. Drinking kava was too important a cultural activity to avoid; in addition, I loved its ritual aspects.

I should have worried more. All of us—Americans, Peace Corps workers, or any regular kava drinker—had diarrhea. I had run out of my usual cure of warm Jello and bouillon, and during that week, I acquired an earnest case of dysentery. This should have been merely an ordinary problem of fieldwork. But the dock strike and our isolation had cut off supplies of toilet paper. I surreptitiously checked the Catholic mission and other places of judicious hoarding. Finally, I found a paperback book, Kurt Vonnegut's *Cat's Cradle,* abandoned by a Peace Corps volunteer. I read a page, tore it out, read another page, and tore it out. I have fondly read that book since, but never with the same utilitarian purpose.

One evening while drinking kava, an old man told me the end of the Lord Kelekel legend:

> One day Lord Kelekel walked up the mountain path to a secluded bathing pool. As he stooped down to enter the water, he chanced to see his reflection in the pool. Horrified at the gray hair and wrinkles of an old man, he committed suicide.

I had been hearing some mild and tactfully phrased complaints about Pernando, one of the interviewers and a high-ranking man from another district. At first, I ignored these reports. But a delegation of serious men came and insisted that action be taken. Pernando was in his middle sixties, a handsome man who looked thirty-five. He had propositioned a widow in the neighborhood who was at least seventy-five years old. I was confused by the gossip. Pohnpeians usually have a high acceptance of geriatric sexuality. Pernando made no secret of his amorous activities during Japanese times or during marital interludes in the American period. He took a lot of teasing, but always cheerfully insisted that he had reformed.

Why, I asked the delegation, should it matter about a little companionship between these two nice old people? I was secretly cheering for the widow. The men of the delegation were indignant. Did I not understand that the moral tone and credibility of this important government project on which I was spending so much money was compromised? Why had I spent months "to help people around the world combat high blood pressure and heart disease" only to sink the project in a love affair? So insistent were they that I sent Pernando back to Kolonia to work with Roger.

After his departure, several of the men who had vociferously objected to his moral transgressions admitted that the widow was a rich woman. Her clanmates, children, and other relatives who would inherit did not want any surprises in the distribution of her land, pigs, and other possessions. This fear, and not morality or impact on the project, accounted for the pressure they brought to bear. Later, at one of the nightly kava poundings, I heard gleeful reports that Pernando's wife had had her revenge. She had summoned all her relatives to his farmstead, killed his pigs, and feasted her kin with his produce.

One morning I did a terrible thing. The air was oppressively heavy; no rain had fallen for several days. I was hot, nauseated, and worried about the details of the project. The delegations of medical personnel and Pohnpeian elders with their contradictory needs had worn me down. Dr. Franko and the factions were enlarging their subtle demands while denying any manipulation. I was sitting on the veranda of my host's house, trying to write field notes, when I saw yet another group of men coming up the path clearly bent on negotiation.

They complained that others had used deception to acquire the contracts for the medical team. They complained about members of the medical team. Then they gossiped about their peers in rival factions. They also made dozens of excuses for why they had not kept their agreement to clear the path to the dispensary. As I listened to them, something snapped.

I stood up on the steps of the porch, a breach of etiquette since my head was above their heads. Each one was older and of higher status and rank than I. They deserved and had always received deference from me. Abandoning public manners, I made a loud speech. I denounced the petty intrigues, the subtle barriers, and the passive resistance. I closed by saying, "I have yet to see a single example of cooperation in this community." Cooperation is probably the most important public value in Pohnpei. This was the same as accusing democracy-loving Americans of being fascists.

What I did is another example of culture shock. This is not to excuse my violation of acceptable public behavior, but only to attempt an explanation. The men I had so loudly addressed left stunned. I felt guilty and worried that I had jeopardized the fragile communications we had achieved.

Less than a week later, several of them returned, beaming. "How right you were to become angry with us. That is how we realized that you are pregnant." I was flabbergasted. Wishing to be modest and not wanting to have my activities restricted, I had told no one but the doctors on the medical team. The men went on to say earnestly that paranoia is the chief symptom of pregnancy in Pohnpei. Pregnant women are allowed to say anything they please, even expected to do so. For one time in their lives they can express anger publicly and make demands on others. Hence, any woman who does this is pregnant. They promised that the path to the dispensary would be cleared and that other acts of cooperation would follow.

In the aftermath of the speech I had given from the veranda and the continuing tensions about money and geriatric sex, I decided to take a field break and let Roger spell me. When he reluctantly arrived, I returned to Kolonia. After a few days of relative relaxation, I made plans to return to Wene on one of the hospital boats.

The hospital aides were several hours late in taking off, so we departed in the late afternoon, after tide had peaked. By the time we reached Madolenihmw (about halfway to our destination under favorable circumstances), the tide was ebbing and darkness had fallen. My uneasiness grew as the aides discussed our location and the strange noises coming from the engine. We seemed clumsy and out of place on the lagoon. A chill wind blew off the ocean, and water sloshed around my feet.

Suddenly the propeller on the outboard motor fell off. One of the aides retrieved it from the shallow lagoon floor. But as we stopped to fix the motor, water filled the bottom of boat at an alarming rate. Without power, we were in danger of drifting into the ocean with the tide. "Bail!" they yelled at me. I searched for one of the bailers made out of Clorox bottles that are usually found on the floor of a boat. There was no bailer. I quickly dumped the tools from a metal box and used it to bail water before we sank. As the lid flapped uselessly and pinched my fingers, I imagined how the news of my senseless death would affect family and friends. I remembered stories of inexperienced Americans dead in foreign lands of exposure or thirst. My fervent imagination omitted only sharks (this was before the movie *Jaws*) from the list of possible causes of death.

The shoreline grew distant as the aides fiddled with the motor. When it started, my hopes of life resumed. It stopped, and my fantasies of death on the lagoon returned. We were making little progress against the tide when I saw a light on the shore. Frightened and increasingly angry, I decided that we should stop there for the night and finish our trip in the morning. When I announced this to the aides, they casually replied, "Oh no, there are ghosts and spirits on that path. We are much safer on the lagoon."

Even though the motor ran intermittently and the danger of drift abated, we were still hours from safety. I was badly chilled. After about an hour, I recognized the boat landing leading into a section of Wapar. "Let's stop here. I know these people and they are gracious hosts. They will understand our need." The aides looked at each other as much as is possible by the light of a half moon. Finally, one of them spoke reluctantly, "That is out of the question. Infamous sorcerers live in that area."

Outraged, I stood up in the boat. "Foreigners cannot be sorcerized. I'm not afraid of sorcery," I announced in English (forgetting my earlier experiences). They placated me and continued to coax the motor. I sat sullenly in the back and refused to speak Pohnpeian for the rest of the trip. I could not believe that any other fears outweighed mine. In assessing blame, I neglected to recognize how well they handled the ailing motor. Their mechanical abilities were greater than their navigational skills. Their fear of things that go bump in the night was greater than the dangers of the lagoon. Eventually, we reached one of the Wene landings. It was late at night and we still had a long walk. In gratitude for my safe arrival, I vowed to forget the tensions in the community.

The members of the medical team did not understood the rival factions or the crosscultural dilemmas of financing the project. They were dependent on us for translation and interpretation of customs. It was difficult to be caught between three cultures: ours, the Pohnpeians', and that of the Australians and New Zealanders. To make matters worse, they had been living and working with each other for twenty-four hours a day. They, too, experienced culture shock, the need for privacy, and the inevitable frictions of close encounters.

On their second Sunday in Wene, they heard that a woman had gone into labor somewhere up in the hills and decided to go to help her. I think they wanted more dramatic medical activity than blood and urine samples. The path led us into a mountainous, sparsely populated region farther away than I had realized. We finally arrived to discover that the pregnant woman had hiked two hours away to her mother's house. Undaunted, Ian, John, and the nurses decided to push on. Reaching our destination at last, we found a relaxed family that had quietly delivered the baby and was surprised to see an international health team.

It is customary for a woman who is about to deliver a baby to go to her mother's house. If she or the infant dies, no one has to worry about possible charges of sorcery. If the husband's family attends the woman and something goes wrong, the gossip and accusations may result in fighting. Sorcery worries surface, and for this reason even the hospital may be safer. During delivery, women are expected to remain stoic and not cry, yell, or make other noises. The family we had walked so far to help reported that the new mother and baby were fine and that she had comported herself well.

As our work in Wene drew mercifully to a close, I felt better and believed that the major problems were behind us. At a meeting of all the Pohnpeian, Australian, New Zealand, and U.S. staff working on the project, we decided to celebrate with a farewell feast. The islanders who worked with us agreed to contribute the yams and kava if the rest of us would purchase the pig. Given the previous difficulties in buying pigs and the money problems in Wene, I should have known better. I believe it would have been easier to negotiate the adoption of a baby than the purchase of a pig.

So began the great pig fiasco. One man agreed to sell his pig for thirty dollars, but when we went up to the farm, he had picked out a 128-pound female porker that he claimed would cost ninety dollars. He raved about her sweet disposition and the status such a fine animal would confer on the medical team. He lamented the loss of her legendary fertility, but was, of course, aware that no honor was too great for our helpful project.

John, the Australian epidemiologist, leaped into the discussion. If this man were so eager to sell a producing female, then something must be wrong with the pig. He examined her with a clinical eye. "Probably sick and certainly too fat to be tasty," he proclaimed. This only increased the pig owner's agitation as pigs dripping with fat are the most desirable. He summoned the neighbors. I left conveniently for other errands, forcing Roger to translate and mediate.

The next morning, I learned that the buyers and seller struck a bargain based on pounds and not on a live pig. The medical team had decided to pay by the pound for a dead pig. In my opinion, this accorded poorly with Pohnpeian custom, but these children of the British Empire had been yearning to deal firmly with the natives. They were certain that reason and common sense among men of good will were more effective than catering to local traditions.

The scene in the dispensary the next morning was awful. In the middle was a pig carcass and a scale. "The price per pound was for dressed pork, not the whole pig," Ian roared. "A pig is a pig. You have to pay for every pound," replied its frustrated owner.

Suddenly an irate and enormous women rushed into the dispensary. None of us knew her. "This is my pig. My brother has no right to sell it," she insisted. She then named an absurdly high price for an indecently dead pig. Everyone had an opinion and a very determined point of view. The members of the medical team who were not exhibiting strains on the composure that made the English empire mighty were worried about leaving the pork in the heat to spoil.

Negotiations about the price started over. This put the purchasers in a bad position since the pig was dead. I had thought that buying a live pig was difficult. Buying a dead one was dreadful. Finally (or so I thought), a price was reached. But the pig owner and his sister suspended their arguments and allied themselves to attack the credibility of the scale. "Those are not Pohnpeian numbers on that scale; it cannot be used to weigh a Pohnpeian pig. How do we know if the scale is rigged or fixed?" they reasoned. This scale arrived by barge from Kolonia, from New Zealand by ship. Now it symbolized the weight of western technology against the defenseless Third World. To the medical team, the scale was an article of faith, an absolute in a shifting world. If you cannot trust a British scale and the metric system, you can trust nothing.

Thank goodness for the tact of Paul Benjamin and Abner Olter, who intervened as neutral parties. Somehow in the muddle of cultural misunderstandings, they brought a resolution to the price of pork. It was not a particularly happy financial solution, as my budget showed, but it averted a pig war, and the medical team had pork to present at their feast.

Far worse were the seven straight meals of pork we ate after the feast. Pork with sugar and soy sauce, pork with yams, fried pork, plain pork. Every swallow was personal.

Roger was also distressed by the lack of communication about money. During the week we ate that dreadful pig, he awakened with a nightmare in which he dreamed that he stood up in church and threw all his money into the air, loudly announcing, "Now you can have all the money. Since I have none to fight over, you will have to take care of me or be discredited for not showing hospitality."

At the farewell feast, the Pohnpeians made lovely speeches about the "ups and downs of human relationships." Several speakers from both highlander and lowlander factions asked us to pardon the mistakes they made. Mutual relief made us friendly. Ian took everyone's blood pressure with his portable machine. He was certain that all our experiences had left us with dangerous high blood pressure. The men who had been most contradictory had the lowest blood pressures. Ian was irritable.

On the morning of our departure from Wene, we all gathered for services at the mission. In his prayer, the lay minister thanked God for giving the Pohnpeian people the strength and courage to cooperate with foreigners.

When we returned to Kolonia, I went straight to Stewo's restaurant and ordered the biggest steak on the menu. As friends watched with amazement, I ordered another one and ate it with relish. In a miracle of international marketing, I found canned whole milk. It tasted just like the real milk that comes out of cartons in the States.

The word of my condition spread rapidly. No one else shared my modesty or reticence about being pregnant. In their view, the baby was already a Pohnpeian. I needed instruction and help. Klarines, Akina, Iseh, Kioko, and the other women who worried about our childlessness and had probably worked fertility spells on me were delighted. Their hopes and chants had been vindicated. They started to organize me in earnest.

I was writing a report on the trip to Wene when I glanced through the droopy screens and saw another delegation, this time of women. As they kicked their zories off at the door, they shouted, "Are you there, little bird's nest?" They carried machetes, mature coconuts, flowers, and other paraphernalia. I was nervous: should I relax, run, or write it all down? Had I agreed to some ritual I knew nothing about? Properly raised, I served cookies and Cokes while they set to work.

Raising the enormous machetes, they halved the coconuts in equal pieces with a gesture I so hopelessly sought to imitate. With the same ease, they scooped out the white meat into a hot skillet. As the heat slowly rendered the coconut into oil, we sat on the floor and talked about pregnancy. The women commented on how well I looked for one so scrawny. They predicted a scrawny baby, too. Several began to share stories about their own pregnancies and deliveries. After skimming the residue floating on top of the hot oil, they added the flowers and stirred. Here was the pure, scented coconut oil essential for ceremonial occasions through uncounted centuries.

Still nervous but fascinated, I watched them bottle the oil. They had obviously made it many times. Then laughing about foreigners, they demanded that I take off most of my clothes and lie on the floor. Embarrassed, I complied. The first midwife, who was giving most of the orders, had trained in midwifery at the district hospital and had years of experience in traditional medicine. Her diagnosis by touch confirmed the twelve-week-old pregnancy. As the second midwife questioned me, she began to pour the warm, scented oil over my body. I relaxed as her strong hands followed the patterns of massage she had learned from generations of island women. While she massaged, she explained that island women know how to prevent the common problems of pregnancy, such as stretch marks, itchy skin, muscular discomfort, or nausea.

Someone else remarked that abortions could also be induced by certain styles of massage and manipulation of the uterus. This method had been used, although rarely, since olden times. They commented on the nausea common in pregnancies of U.S. women and assured me that I would have no more. Having heard about my paranoia and anger in Wene, they complimented me on acting like a Pohnpeian woman and encouraged me to vent my feelings anytime I pleased. During pregnancy, I had every right to get mad and tell people off.

As the midwife worked, the women talked. They discussed the stages of pregnancy and labor and how the mother's attitudes affect the personality of the child. They explained how I would feel, emotionally and physically, at each new development. Some of the information was technical and medical. Nothing I heard contradicted the western view of biological processes nor violated common sense for childbearing. Beyond the practical, however, was a wisdom and sharing I had yet to encounter in my own culture.

In the United States at that time, impersonal doctors and nurses in secretive medical settings treated pregnancy like an illness. On occasion, echoes of Victorianism or fears of midwifery surfaced. The childbirth these Pohnpeian women and their ancestors had experienced was an aberration in my native land. They had never read the research that indicates that women instructed in the physiology, anatomy, and psychology of birth and encouraged by age mates and peers have easier deliveries and better bonding with their babies. But this was clearly the message they wanted me to hear.

They left me with the oil and instructions for its use. They were right. It does everything they claimed. How can I describe the intensity and delights of the massages? My body tingled for weeks. The concept of sisterhood, so prominent in the women's movement in the United States, was exemplified by my Pohnpeian prenatal group. I often remember how much they taught me. I understand the appeal of midwives and skilled family members caring for pregnant and postpartum women.

A woman's world I had rarely seen in Pohnpei opened to me. In this world, women are confident, noisy, supportive, and knowledgeable. They live in their bodies. Pregnancy, nursing, and making love are all points in a sensual continuum. As they lay out the dead for burial, they hope for the quickening of childbirth. Women are related through clans, through dangers shared, and through the knowledge that the circle of life and death closes in their bodies. In the presence of men or in public, these same women are deferential in a double standard.

I continued to marvel at and finally to enjoy the attention I received. Men stopped me on the roads and expressed delight about all pregnancies and babies. My status among the islanders soared. However, when I mentioned my prenatal classes to Americans, they were distressed. The women were upset that I was in the hands of native midwives rather than "real" doctors. Some American men were uncomfortable with my pregnancy and seemed to regard the process as a disease that lowered my I.Q. I assumed that my experiences were not valid to share with Americans and peers. Only later did I see what happened as data for anthropology and acceptable for discussion.

To satisfy my curiosity and the demands of Americans that I have proper checkups, I attended one of the prenatal clinics at the hospital. I picked a clinic day attended mainly by outisland women from the Polynesian atoll of Kapingamarangi. Contrary to the stereotype of maidenly beauty painted by Gaugain, the Polynesian women were each at least six feet tall and over 200 pounds. In vividly colored, ruffled dresses, these women overpowered the activities of the clinic. They fussed over me: "So short and thin, no bulge to show. Could she really be pregnant?" Questioning me thoroughly, they agreed among themselves that I was not faking. Talking all at once and hugging me occasionally, they recounted boisterous stories of pregnancy and childbirth with some sexy tales as footnotes. I wallowed in mellow bliss. With so much acceptance and nurturance, I wanted to be pregnant forever. These women appeared to feel the same way. They certainly had lots of babies. From my new viewpoint, the clinic was a roaring success. True to form for western medical care, I had a long wait, a short exam, and a prescription for vitamin pills.

Roger was entranced with our future baby. In the meantime, though, he and Jack did not want to miss a great anthropological opportunity for collecting data. Roger wanted spells, chants, ingredients, symptomatology, schedules for treatments, and other technical features of indigenous medicine. He reasoned that I was in a much better position to collect this information than he. Jack wrote to congratulate

us and by the second sentence outlined a research project for me. I was to explore
the relationship between mythology, social structure, and reality on Pohnpei as
revealed through conception and childbirth. Remember Lord Kelekel, he insisted,
magically born and reputed to be the offspring of the Thunder God and his clanmate
(perhaps his sister). The God of Thunder somehow made her pregnant with sour
citrus fruit or raw fish.

Neither believed me when I extolled the virtues of coconut oil, massage, and
female support systems. Nor were they interested in lectures I had received on
the customs of catering to the every whim of a pregnant women. Pohnpeian
husbands and relatives are expected to arise in the middle of the night and fix
the foods a pregnant woman craves and needs for the baby's growth. Attention
to the arbitrary and strong-minded desires of a pregnant wife takes precedence
over regular routines and career advancement and should increase with birth and
continue during nursing. I never did convince them that no woman really believes
in magical sources of pregnancy, that the Lord Kelekel's legend was irrelevant
to this new reality, or that the traditional medical practices really centered on basic
biological information, shared experiences, and the love of babies.

The Pohnpeian women were not finished with my training. We had to discuss
names for the baby, its gender, its date of birth, and pertinent aspects of its
personality and rearing. They taught me how to determine the sex of the baby
by feeling the position of the backbone. This can only be done in the last few
months, when the baby has determined its own sex and assumes the correct posture.
If the spine rests on the right, it will be a boy; on the left, a girl.

We consulted a diviner from Yap (another island in Micronesia). He had an
elaborate system of number divination based on the safe and dangerous positions
in a canoe. He drew a diagram of the cross bars of a single outrigger and wrote
the question to be answered. He made supposedly random series of marks from
which he devised a series of two-digit combinations of the numbers 1, 2, 3, and
4. Certain numbers in key positions on the canoe drawing are auspicious. We had
asked two questions. On the first, about the sex of the infant, he predicted a boy
baby (as did all the divination techniques, including the backbone method). As
a future mother, I believed that the divination was not objective and that the diviner
revealed what he believed Americans and Pohnpeians wanted to hear. As an
anthropologist, I see these predictions, not as fancy and superstition, but as a form
of caring and attention that a society invests in its offspring and in parenting.

The other question was more pressing. Roger wanted to know if his father, who
was bedridden with a broken hip, would be strong again. He feared that the family
had withheld the truth, not wishing to worry us. The omens were highly favorable
and, indeed, his father's hip mended without trouble.

The project was nearing an end. I had to return to teaching and would not be
able to give birth among the women of the island. We calculated the date of birth
as May 16. They explained carefully that the baby would be born during high tide
on that day. This precipitated a lively discussion on the relativity of tidal movements

in Louisiana and Pohnpei. The midwives suggested that I study the moon and question navigators to determine high tide. I told them about television weather reports.

We compared labor and delivery practices. They knew about but disapproved of the U.S. custom of allowing strangers and men to attend a woman in labor. "You mean that your own mother or sister or aunts are forbidden to help you?" Delivery was the one time at which privacy was valued by the Pohnpeians. Women feared that strangers would report a lapse of courage. In giving birth, women must show bravery and suppress cries of pain. Female relatives encouraged quiet behavior and offered gentle support.

During these sessions, sandwiched between the preparations for our departure, they explained the ceremony called "mother's milk," which follows the birth of a baby, particularly the first one. Relatives make a small feast to insure that the new mother will have enough milk to feed the baby. One of the Catholic priests who lived for many years on Pohnpei interpreted this custom as a mere formality. The families did not necessarily feel that a feast aids in effective breast-feeding, but rather it is done out of social pressure and to avoid criticism. He admitted that such customs bring families together and cement a marriage. One of the functions of such a ceremony is to identify the father publicly and commit him and his family to the newborn.

But the explanation of women who had nursed babies was different. Imagine the distress, they said, of giving birth to a much desired child and not being able to feed it. No baby bottles existed in ancient times, and accepting a surrogate nursing mother would be the same as adoption. Akina and Klarines showed me how to shave the top of a drinking coconut to make a substitute baby bottle. Some of the women told me stories about keeping babies alive with coconut milk. I had often seen women chewing bits of banana and taro to place in the mouths of babies.

Since then, I have seen research showing that the more social support and attention a new mother receives during the hours, days, and weeks after a birth, the better off she and her infant will be. This is particularly true for young or inexperienced mothers. Even monkeys and apes, which presumably feel little pressure for social conformity to custom, are particularly attentive to a new mother. Rather than isolating women as is usually done in the United States, people in many other cultures treat birth as the occasion to reward women for their contributions and to perform rituals that strengthen the social networks. I was sorry to miss the mother's milk ceremony. My women friends insisted that I could find someone in the States to conduct the ritual, but I never did.

I had learned to admire their habits of child rearing and tried to imagine how these customs could fit with the West's more rigid beliefs. Toilet training is accomplished easily, as all the members of the family encourage the baby. Since babies are not dressed, even in a diaper, it is easy to discern their intentions and clean up their messes. Many mothers begin training their babies by grunting for the infant to defecate and hissing or blowing on its genitals to signal urination.

They said that anyone can tell when a baby is going to urinate or defecate and hold it away from them over the edge of a porch or on a path. Perhaps the mother's learned skills are more impressive than the infant's. To me, such habits showed the close attention of the caretakers to the baby's needs and behaviors. When the baby starts to walk, all the caretakers tell it to go outside, and eventually the infant learns the tricks. When I tried these lessons in the United States with my new baby, I was roundly criticized.

Life with a baby was so easy for them. Someone was always there to carry and sleep with it. With no carpets or furniture to protect and no diapers to wash, the physical labor of child rearing was simple. Babies adjust to the schedules of all the people who constantly surround them, rather than the reverse. Child rearing, to the Pohnpeians as to many other people of the world, is not what a mother does. It is the activity and responsibility of relatives and the culture at large. Pohnpeian mothers still scream at their children and spank them occasionally. So do other family members. A mother's efforts are duplicated by everyone. As Pohnpeians say, "These are all our children."

The kinship system and the words used for relatives make the "mother" just one of many. Grandmothers, sisters, and aunts are also mothers, extending the range of a child's security. There is less concern with "things," the paraphernalia of childhood. Children do not need toys; they need interaction. People are their playground. Men pick them up and blow on their tummies. Siblings play finger games. Others tease and sing to them. The constant social interaction that marks adult life begins in infancy. Babies sleep in the middle of the floor with the rest of the family. They are constantly carried, played with, and attended. I always marveled how their lives differed from those of babies in the United States, who are dressed in layers, deposited in assorted pieces of furniture from cribs to car seats, and frequently left alone (although confined). A variety of toys and objects, rather than people, mark the earliest years of U.S. babies. I also marveled at the public presence of island children. What few temper tantrums they threw were easily managed and rarely repeated. They did not make scenes or dominate conversations.

The spatial arrangements within a Pohnpeian household offer intimacy and none of the physical privacy of middle-class homes in the States. With the entire family occupying the same space, children's bad dreams or separation anxieties are easily resolved. Bedtimes and the desires of children to sleep with others are not issues. These children witness sex acts without apparent consequences. Mothers can nurse their babies without interrupting sleep and other activities. Children sleep together. Incest and incest fantasies occur no more regularly in this atmosphere than in the closeted U.S. society. In the States, individual mothers fear social censure if their children disturb others or make messes. On Pohnpei, kids cannot ruin carpets, mark on walls, spot upholstery, or break very much. There are fewer dangers and more caregivers.

Americans like to believe that they are permissive, understanding, even child-centered. In contrast to the Pohnpeians and others I have studied throughout the world, they appear to demand a rigid, difficult set of achievements early in life. People in the United States are trained for individualism, not for group adjustment. Newborns are put alone in a bedroom to sleep. The Pohnpeians have a folk saying, "You didn't just grow up." They believe that the actions and attention of many people consciously caring is the reason kids grow. The whole island and the kin group, not just the mother, are responsible for nurturing a child to adulthood.

In any event, Westerners are not growing more like Pohnpeians in the way they raise children, whatever the apparent advantages. Instead, Pohnpeians are becoming more like western families. The nuclear family will become more common than the extended family. In the past, the need for cooperation with family members kept the young married couple subjected to the lineage and to the kindred. Today, the cash economy has made it possible, even necessary, for families to be independent. In some families, obligations to siblings are less important to a man as wives become more important. Women are increasingly responsible for budgeting and earning money. Younger, educated wives are working outside their homes and may support themselves and their families while contributing as a man does to the extended family.

A wife's task is more difficult than in the past. Like me and many of my friends, they have two full-time jobs. Schools remove the older children and potential helpers from the home much of the time. Women cannot easily recruit helpers and babysitters. The double standard still persists, and for women work is harder to find and harder to keep than for men.

I knew that the United States was not a place to raise a child in the Pohnpeian manner. I would not automatically find an atmosphere of gentle acceptance and sociability. But with the departure of the medical team, the project was drawing to a close, and our time for leaving neared. We worked hard to finish up the bits and pieces of research just as our language skills and ease of movement were giving us new energy. New topics to study opened up. There was so much I wanted to do. All fieldworkers feel this yearning to stay. The learning is always so incomplete.

I was ambivalent about returning to the States. The war in Vietnam was still raging and campus unrest had not abated. I had to return to the materialism and domination of possessions that I had happily left behind. Where in the States could I find hours of gentle training, offers of sisterly support, a public acceptance of pregnancy and lactation, and spectacular massages? Would my baby ever experience the freedom and the limits of an extended family?

The last two months we spent in Pohnpei centered on the formalities of leaving. Roger and I made an honor feast to the Paramount Chief of U, as title holders are expected to do every year. The interviewers, friends, and families with whom we had shared so much gave us enormous farewell feasts and many presents. We mailed off the last packages of data for the computer in North Carolina. Having arrived with three suitcases between us, we now had to dispose of a household of possessions, a bike, a kerosene refrigerator, two cats, and a dog.

On the last morning, I hiked up a high hill overlooking the town and the harbor to watch the sun rise. I smelled coconut husk fires on the air and heard a distant pounding of someone washing clothes. I did not plan to tell this tale then.

The Pohnpeians who shared so much with me do not end their stories with "they lived happily ever after." Thrice-told tales are never simple or naive. Just as they embellish yams and tales with the green leaves of camouflage, they end them with this warning:

> You who hear my tale should listen very carefully and straighten it out for yourself. Sometimes what I say is not straight.

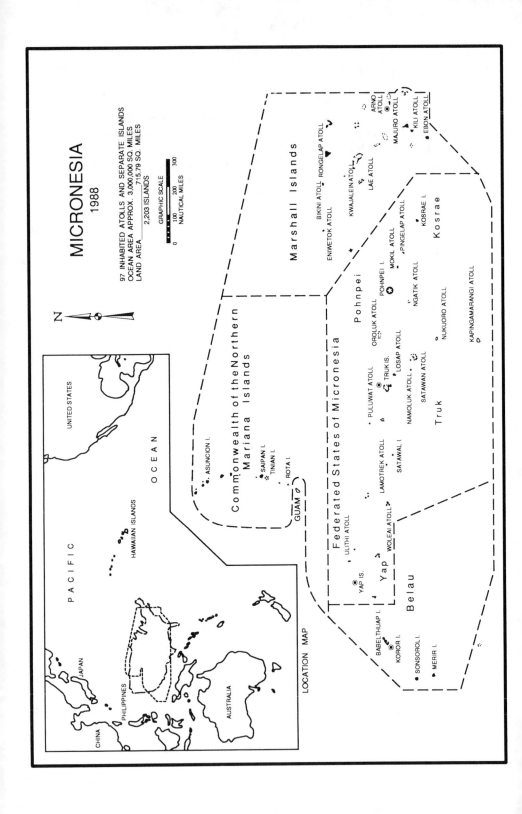

MICRONESIA
1988

97 INHABITED ATOLLS AND SEPARATE ISLANDS
OCEAN AREA APPROX. 3,000,000 SQ. MILES
LAND AREA   715.79 SQ. MILES
2,203 ISLANDS

GRAPHIC SCALE

0   100   200   300
NAUTICAL MILES

N

UNITED STATES

PACIFIC

OCEAN

HAWAIIAN ISLANDS

CHINA

JAPAN

PHILIPPINES

AUSTRALIA

LOCATION MAP

Commonwealth of the Northern
Mariana Islands

• ASUNCION I.

☆ SAIPAN I.
• TINIAN I.
• ROTA I.

GUAM ◁

Federated States of Micronesia

ULITHI ATOLL

YAP IS.

Y a p

WOLEAI ATOLL

Belau

BABELTHUAP I.
KOROR I.

• SONSOROL I.
• MERIR I.

LAMOTREK ATOLL

SATAWAL I.

PULUWAT ATOLL

OROLUK ATOLL

TRUK IS.

LOSAP ATOLL

NAMOLUK ATOLL
SATAWAN ATOLL

T r u k

NUKUORO ATOLL

KAPINGAMARANGI ATOLL

P o h n p e i

POHNPEI I.

MOKIL ATOLL
PINGELAP ATOLL

NGATIK ATOLL

KOSRAE I.

K o s r a e

Marshall Islands

BIKINI ATOLL   RONGELAP ATOLL

ENIWETOK ATOLL

KWAJALEIN ATOLL

LAE ATOLL

ARNO
ATOLL

MAJURO ATOLL

KILI ATOLL

EBON ATOLL

Since Then

A ll the Pohnpeian prognostications about the gender of our child were wrong. She has been, since birth, a lovely girl. But the predictions of timing were accurate. She was born at high tide on the morning of May 15—I remembered to subtract one day from their predictions of May 16 when I crossed the International Date Line. They were also right about the joys of raising a child. In returning to the United States and its impersonal, bureaucratic, technology-centered customs of giving birth, I sorely missed the warmth and human knowledge I had found while pregnant on a tropical island.

Fieldwork and the stresses of building dual careers are hard on professional marriages. Roger and I are divorced, but together we treasure our daughter. I am indebted to him for his insights on curing, rituals of forgiveness, and much more, both before and since.

On May 16, 1985, Dr. John (Jack) L. Fischer died suddenly of a heart attack. The irony of his death and my grief is compounded by the fact that I had just begun this story and was sorting our correspondence. Jack was an anthropologist of extraordinary breadth and depth who knew more about Pohnpei than any foreigner ever. There is still much more I want to ask him.

Trite as it sounds, living on the island changed my life. When I think about teenage pregnancy, adoption, incest, childbirth, head lice, the homeless, the elderly, peeping Toms, sex, sensuality, toilet training, or a hundred other topics, I wonder how other cultures define and handle these. What would the Pohnpeians do? Sometimes these questions have answers that I try to communicate to my students.

I maintain contact with the island in various ways. Once, a group of Pohnpeians on a State Department tour connected with the status elections visited me in my home. Barely greeting me at the front door, they rushed past to pick up "our baby" and did not put her down for the remainder of their stay. They reported on the political struggles, the deaths and successions to high titles, the growth of alcoholism, crime and suicide. Their only request was to visit an Indian reservation to see how those of a different color and culture were treated in the United States. They also reported that shortly after I had left, my fat dog had been eaten at a feast given by my adopted extended family to whom he belonged.

Lately, the news from Pohnpei centers on the completion of the road around the island. Although it is unpaved and will wash out in the frequent rains, the road means that communities like Wene are no longer remote. Commuting to work is now a fact of life. Other changes will go up and down that road. For good and bad, life in the rural areas looks more like life in Kolonia and life in Kolonia looks more like an outpost of poor America.

Kava still tastes like slimy mud. Kolonia has kava bars where anyone can buy a cup and ignore the etiquette of drinking it. The talk about bottling it and marketing it in the United States has progressed to a more serious level. I hope they do. I miss that bitter pepper beverage and the grace of pounding it. I wonder what kind of market there is for a drink that causes a temporary paralysis of the legs, numbs the mouth, dulls the appetite, lowers the blood pressure, and tastes like mildewed boiled okra. Perhaps Kava Lite?

Kolonia remains crowded; the housing shortage is acute. The architectural style of the town is still characterized by four-by-eight sheets of plywood, rippled tin, and mounds of trash. More and more Pohnpeians are living off the island or spend years away from their natal home. Missionaries and shipwrecked sailors are not the only people to bring foreign ways to Pohnpei. Now returning sons and daughters bring back foreign traditions as part of their own life. This may have more impact than colonialism ever had.

I hear that young couples hold hands and eat together in public. Dating customs are changing. Young people who have gone off the island return wanting movies, restaurants, bars, and a separate young adult life-style. It is said that girls exchange sexual favors for a night out dancing. Young men are feeling some pressure to be engaged and get serious.

Parents pay relatives for babysitting. Young people with good educations cannot find employment. There are disturbing reports of drug use. Worries about the future of their children, the loss of custom, and the seductiveness of foreign ways continue. Pohnpeians must adjust to growing numbers of foreigners and to outislanders who claim Pohnpeian citizenship and kinship without full participation in the title and feasting systems.

The obligations of feasting have accelerated. The basins full of cooked foods and consumer goods are now an ordinary sight under feast house roofs. The products of the land—yams, pigs, and breadfruit—must be matched by the products of wage labor and commercialism. A favorite interpretation of the growth of this basin customs is that this reflects the vitality of Pohnpeian culture in keeping alive the traditional systems by incorporating new elements. The same themes of respect for tradition and high people, cooperation, redistribution, prestige striving, and conspicuous consumption remain vital. Islanders still argue about the expense of their contributions to feasts. I like to think that in the olden times, some Pohnpeians lamented the labor to build Nan Madol, complained about the Lords of Deleur, griped about those messy, noisy pigs that had just arrived, accused their peers of incest or sorcery, struggled against speaking high language, and gave more to a feast than they took home.

I now suspect that the large federal grant on blood pressure and heart disease reflected more the concerns of bureaucrats in Washington than it did a concern for pure research or the health problems of a faraway island. Heart attacks are a sad cliche for the men who control the money.

The research on blood pressure and heart disease has been scarcely published in technical sources. The data were so extensive that full publication may never be possible. Dr. John Cassel and others who applied for the research grant died too soon. I regret that we have yet to find a way to relate these findings, however esoteric, to the lives of ordinary people.

We learned that the sedentary and overweight women of the island have higher blood pressure than men do. This was an unexpected result, and the hypotheses, which had been formulated about men in industrial societies, did little to account for this. On the other hand, sadly enough, blood pressures on Pohnpei have begun to rise with age, changes in diet, and the pace of modernization. Heart attacks and cardiovascular diseases are more frequently reported.

The folk wisdom of Pohnpei was largely right. Life in Kolonia forced changes not only in life-styles but in bodily behaviors. When men and women no longer engage in the active exercise of walking everywhere and managing a farmstead, where they eat canned and processed foods with higher fat and salt contents, rather than the low-sodium diets of their forebears, where they hold sedentary jobs, drink more alcohol and less kava, the subtle changes that blood pressure measures are evident. Two factors stand out: where high blood pressure is present, weight gain and increased salt intake are correlated.

On the other hand, we learned that Pohnpeians have excellent coping mechanisms for the stresses of modern life. There is much that could be learned from them. They continue to promote their networks of family, friends, and social institutions, both traditional and modern, which give meaning and structure to their lives. As we anticipated, it is not stress, worry, or hard times alone that produce health problems. It is being trapped in them with no help from others, no recourse in thought or action to alleviate their harsh effects.

There are many ways to tell a story. My colleagues in epidemiology and public health who use very sophisticated computers and data analysis techniques to report research results are sometimes reluctant to make statements about the real world. They want narrow categories and definitive (perhaps boring) statistics. They do not live with their subjects, nor listen to and speak the language of others different from themselves. To anthropologists, a part of the real world is our observations and our participation in events which, if quantified and measured, would lose their meaning. During the years I spent with this project, I worked and lived in these two different worlds of knowledge. I chose the values and language of anthropology to tell this story. Other ways of seeing are equally valid.

In 1947, the United Nations designated Micronesia as the Trust Territory of the Pacific Islands. The agreement with the United States declared the area "a strategic trust," which gave the United States wide latitude for military activities with oversight by the U.N. Security Council and the U.N. Trusteeship Council. When I worked there, most of the discussions assumed a unified future with the island chains of Micronesia linked to the United States in some kind of independence (free association, compact, commonwealth, or other status).

After 1975, status negotiations grew more and more complex. People argued over the legalities and interpretations of the original trusteeship agreements. The public negotiations were only the tip of a vast iceberg of gossip, infighting, putative deals, and political rhetoric.

In 1977, the format of the negotiations between the U.S. government and the people of Micronesia about governance grew more complex as Palau and the Marshalls began negotiating separately from the other islands. After angry words, intermittent acts of courage, and several elections, the former Trust Territory split into smaller geographic chains of islands. The island groups of Micronesia had never had political unity or a common self-government. They were divided by languages, ethnic rivalries, distant ecologies and different histories. Everybody — nations, islands, individuals, and observers — had their own needs, ideologies, and agendas. The negotiating power that unity had given them was lost.

After plebiscites, approvals, amendments, revisions, and political maneuvering, the Congress of the Federated States of Micronesia passed a resolution of acceptance for the Compact of Free Association document in March, 1986. Following that, the United Nations and the United States formally ended the trusteeship.

As a result, Pohnpei has become the capital of the Federated States of Micronesia (FSM), a still partially dependent island country. The FSM will include four states: Kosrae, Pohnpei, Truk, and Yap (see map). Kolonia, with its one paved road, is the capital's major urban center.

The Compact of Free Association allows each state in the FSM some autonomy in both domestic and foreign affairs, but the United States maintains responsibility for and control of defense. The United States is willing to pay for Micronesia's strategic location. For the Federated States of Micronesia, with its Pohnpeian capital, the compact grants them sovereignty, self-government, and approximately two billion dollars in operating funds and capital improvement grants over the fifteen years of the pact. The Marshall Islands have a similar Free Association Compact. The Mariana Islands are a commonwealth, and the political future of the republic of Belau (Palau Islands) is still undecided. Like other postcolonial nations, the Pohnpeians changed the spelling of their island's name to project a new feeling of independence.

Political realities, along with consumerism, television, tourism, and increased communication outside the island will irrevocably alter the lives of the Pohnpeians. Pohnpei continues to change rapidly, much to the dismay of those who, like some in U.S. society, believe that at a golden age in the past everything worked better, children obeyed their elders, and the customs had more power. Anthropologists who have worked on this lovely island continue to be impressed with the vitality and cohesion of the culture. They have wonderful stories and insights to share. At the same time, a new generation of Micronesians is ready to tell its own tales of life upon the stone altar.

Additional Readings

Bascom, William R. 1965. Ponape: A Pacific economy in transition. *Anthropological Records*. Vol. 22. Berkeley: University of California Press.

As an early work in applied anthropology, this monograph, written in 1946, outlines the resources and economy and recommends programs for United States development in the proposed new Trust Territory.

_____. 1948. Ponapean prestige economy. *Southwestern Journal of Anthropology* [now called *Journal of Anthropological Research*], 4(3):211-21. (Reprinted in *Cultures of the Pacific: Selected Readings*. Edited by Thomas G. Harding and Ben J. Wallace. New York: Free Press, 1970.)

This article is still as topical and relevant as the day it was written.

Cassel, John, Ralph Patrick, and David Jenkins. 1960. Epidemiological analysis of the health implications of culture change: A conceptual model. *Annals of the New York Academy of Sciences* 84(17):919-38.

Cassel, John, and Herman Tyroler. 1961. Epidemiological studies of culture change: I. Health status and recency of industrialization. *Archives of Environmental Health* 3:25-33.

_____. 1964. Health consequences of culture change: II. The effect of urbanization on coronary heart mortality in rural residents. *Journal of Chronic Diseases* 17:167-77.

This small sample of John Cassel's research and theoretical approaches formed the basis for the Pohnpei Blood Pressure and Social Change Project.

Fischer, Ann M. 1970. Fieldwork in five cultures. A chapter in *Women in the Field*. Edited by Peggy Golde. Chicago: Aldine.

A delightful account of Ann Fischer's life and work in Truk, Pohnpei, and other places.

157

Fischer, John L. 1970. Adoption on Ponape. *Adoption in Eastern Oceania.* Edited by Vern
Carroll. Honolulu: University of Hawaii Press.
One of Fischer's many good basic articles, this one is part of a volume comparing
adoption practices in other cultures of Oceania.
———. 1969. Honorific speech and social structure: A comparison of Japanese and
Ponapean. *Journal of the Polynesian Society* 78(3):417-22.
———. 1966. A Ponapean Oedipus tale, a structural and sociopsychological analysis. *Journal
of American Folklore* 79(311):109-29. Reprinted in *The Anthropologist Looks at Myth.*
Compiled by Melville Jacobs, and edited by John Greenway. Austin: University of
Texas Press, 1966.
The above two articles are fascinating analyses of Pohnpeian intellectual life.
Fischer, John L. with the assistance of Ann M. Fischer. 1957. The Eastern Carolines.
Behavior Science Monographs. New Haven, Connecticut: Human Relations Area Files.
A descriptive ethnography of Truk and Pohnpei done in the George Peter Murdock
HRAF style.
Fischer, John L., Ann M. Fischer, and Frank J. Mahony. 1959. Totemism and allergy.
International Journal of Social Psychiatry 5(1):33-40.
Will breaking clan taboos on eating certain foods cause guilty people to have allergic
reactions? Data from Pohnpei suggest connections.
Fischer, John L., Saul H. Riesenberg, and Marjorie G. Whiting, eds. and trans. 1977. *Luelen
Bernart: The Book of Luelen.* Pacific Science Series, no. 8. Canberra: Australian
National University Press.
The Luelen manuscript in its edited and translated form is a compelling oral history
of Pohnpei. Luelen, a prominent Pohnpeian who died at the end of World War II,
includes place names, myths, legends, botanical lore, and advice.
Fischer, John L., Roger L. Ward, and Martha C. Ward. 1976. Ponapean conceptions of
incest. *The Journal of Polynesian Society* 85(2)199-207.
The results of our little study were published in a special issue on incest prohibitions
in Micronesia and Polynesia.
Garvin, Paul L., and Saul H. Riesenberg. 1952. Respect behavior on Ponape: An
ethnolinguistic study. *American Anthropologist* 54(2):201-20.
This article is important to Pohnpeian ethnography, but is even more significant for
the fields of sociolinguistics and ethnolinguistics.
Hanlon, David L. 1988. *Upon a Stone Altar: A History of the Island of Pohnpei to 1890.*
Pacific Islands Monograph Series, no. 5. Honolulu: University of Hawaii Press.
The reader can decide whether this book is excellent history or impressive anthropology.
The author is a former Peace Corps volunteer whom I am delighted to have known
on Pohnpei.
Hambruch, Paul. 1932-1936. Ponape. *Ergebnisse der Sudsee-Expedition 1908-1910.* Edited
by G. Thilenius. Hamburg. 1932-1936.
A German scientific expedition went into Micronesia before World War I. Volume
7 (subvolumes 1, 2, and 3) is about Pohnpei, its history, Nan Madol, myths, and general
ethnography (at the turn of the century).

Hughes, Daniel T., and Sherwood G. Lingenfelter, eds. 1974. *Political Development in Micronesia*. Columbus, Ohio: Ohio State University Press.
This is a very necessary book for understanding the history and politics of Micronesia under U.S. administration.

Lieber, Michael D. 1984. Strange feast: Negotiating identities on Ponape. *Journal of the Polynesian Society* 93.
This is an important article on the ethnic groups of Pohnpei, the outislanders, and how Pohnpeians use the title and feasting systems to define their identities on the island.

O'Connell, James F. 1972. *A Residence of Eleven Years in New Holland and the Caroline Islands*. Edited by Saul H. Riesenberg. Pacific History Series, no. 4. Honolulu: The University Press of Hawaii.
A lying, shipwrecked ex-convict lives and marries on Pohnpei, leaving a lively journal that is skillfully sorted out by the extraordinarily careful research of Riesenberg.

Patrick, R.C., I.A.M. Prior, J.C. Smith, and A.H. Smith. 1983. Relationship between blood pressure and modernity among Ponapeans. *International Journal of Epidemiology* 12:36-44.
Ten years after the end of the Pohnpei Blood Pressure and Social Change Project, a technical article on the results of the physical examinations appeared. I had a hard time finding the project in the article.

Petersen, Glenn. 1982. *One Man Cannot Rule a Thousand: Fission in a Ponapean Chiefdom*. Ann Arbor: University of Michigan Press.
This book is a tight analysis of political processes in a section (Awak) of the district of U. Petersen's work is particularly instructive for the functioning of modern chiefdoms.

―――. 1979. External politics, internal politics, and Ponapean social formation. *American Ethnologist* 6:25-40.
This article analyzes Pohnpeian economic development and argues that colonial experiences have not produced a typical peasant society. In common with most anthropologists who have worked Pohnpei, Petersen maintains that Pohnpeians have retained most of their lands, precontact subsistance, and even modified their native polity.

Riesenberg, Saul H. 1968. *The Native Polity of Ponape*. Vol. 10 of the Smithsonian Contributions to Anthropology. Washington, D.C.: Smithsonian Institution Press.
Riesenberg was Curator of Pacific Ethnography at the Smithsonian. He did the fieldwork for this volume in 1947-1948. So painstaking, elaborate and definitive is this book that Pohnpeians often quote from it or ask what Riesenberg had to say about a ceremony or a custom.

Riesenberg, Saul H., and John L. Fischer. 1955. Some Ponapean Proverbs. *Journal of American Folklore* 68:217-27.
Anthropologists have long used their classic interpretations of oral literature on Pohnpei.

Rehg, Kenneth L., and Damian G. Sohl. 1979. *Ponapean-English Dictionary*. Honolulu: The University Press of Hawaii.

―――. 1981. *Ponapean Reference Grammar*. Honolulu: The University Press of Hawaii.
At last, here is an excellent grammar, dictionary, and standardized orthography (without a few place-name spelling changes). The authors are native speakers of Pohnpeian who had good help from the university of Hawaii and the East-West Center, as well as from previous compilers of short dictionaries.

Van Maanen, John. 1988. *Tales of the Field: On Writing Ethnography.* Chicago: University of Chicago Press.
Here is a provocative stimulus to social scientists, students, or professionals whose stories beg to be told.

About the Author

Dr. Martha C. Ward is Professor of Anthropology and Urban and Regional Studies at the University of New Orleans. She is the author of *Them Children: A Study in Language Learning* (Holt, Rinehart and Winston, 1971; Waveland Press, 1986) and *Poor Women, Powerful Men: America's Great Experiment in Family Planning* (Westview Press, 1986). She is also conducting research on sexual decision making, women in poverty, urban health, and parenting under pressure.